Retail Banking
3rd edition

Keith Pond, Ph.D., FCIB, FHEA

Senior Lecturer in Banking and Economics,
Loughborough University

GLOBAL
professional
publishing

Global Professional Publishing Ltd
Random Acres
Slip Mill Lane
Hawkhurst
Cranbrook
Kent TN18 5AD
Email: publishing@gppbooks.com

ISBN 978-1-906403-98-0

Printed in the United Kingdom by 4Edge

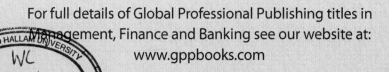

For full details of Global Professional Publishing titles in Management, Finance and Banking see our website at:
www.gppbooks.com

Table of Contents

Preface
to 3rd edition

My main aim in writing and updating this text is to provide a basic introduction to retail banking and to give the book an international appeal.

The text draws on the inspiration provided by *The Business of Banking* that I co-wrote and updated with Geoff Lipscombe in 1998 and 2002. Retail banks have undergone considerable changes in the last twenty years, their capacity to react to economic, environmental, political, social and technological pressures will guarantee further changes in the decades to come. This text substantially revises the earlier versions of the book in its treatment of issues surrounding the industry in Section A. The text also emphasises the priorities of retail banks today and their regulatory and practical environment in Section B.

The text itself is divided into two sections – Sections A and Section B – covering banking concepts and the current banking environment and key retail banking operations respectively.

Section A considers what banking actually is and what banks do. Some key economic concepts that underpin much banking activity are discussed in both historical and modern-day contexts. Banking risks are examined as are some of the ways in which banks overcome or minimise the adverse impact of such risks. The section goes on to review the position of banks in the economy, their regulation by national and international bodies and looks at bank profitability from the perspective of bank annual accounts.

Section B covers the key banking transactions, from the basic contract between the banker and customer via the different types of bank account and product offered to the use of payment systems (a necessary adjunct to intermediation). The section goes on to introduce the topic of lending, where some key credit risk tools are reviewed and applied and basic securities, a vital "secondary repayment method" if credit default occurs.

In both sections it is necessary to focus on particular examples of practice in their own national and regulatory environments. Often the differences in law, history and geography result in different banking responses to familiar questions and challenges. This text cannot promise to be an exhaustive review of all practice but uses specific examples to highlight generic principles and common responses to them. Often the default setting is UK and EU practice as much international law has been inherited by Imperial connections in former times.

Particular attention is drawn to the "Further reading and web-links" sections at the end of each chapter. The texts and links cited are widely available and often provide more detailed coverage, or specific examples, of the topics in the chapters themselves.

Whilst I have made every effort to ensure that the information contained in the text is accurate and up to date errors will remain and I take full responsibility for them. Feedback on the text is welcomed.

Keith Pond
Loughborough
January 2014

Disclaimer

Throughout the text reference is made to fictitious organisations including "Countryside Bank plc" and "Riverside Bank Pte Limited". These organisations are pure inventions by the author and any resemblance to any organisation carrying these names or any similar names is purely coincidental.

Dedication

To Judy

First, last and always. My inspiration for everything I do.

Acknowledgements

I am grateful to the School of Business and Economics at Loughborough University for allowing re-publication of materials previously used in teaching at that institution.

Section A

CHAPTER 1

The Retail Banking Environment

Objectives

After studying this chapter you should be able to:

▶ Describe the environments within which retail banks operate in a number of countries.

▶ Outline the key Political, Legal and Economic issues that impact on bank strategies.

▶ Outline the key Social and Technological issues that help to frame trends in retail banking.

▶ Explain what this book is all about.

Introduction

This opening chapter in Section A describes the environment within which retail banks operate. It starts by outlining what a retail bank is and what it does. The chapter goes on to show a PEST[1] analysis of retail banking, drawing together a number of themes from different countries around the world, most of which are to be expanded upon in later chapters.

Key drivers for change during the last 30 years have been regulation and technology. The focus in the immediate aftermath of the credit-crunch of 2007/08 is also regulation. To this analysis are added the areas of macroeconomics, competition and sociological features, including ethical and "green" issues.

Although the chapter reviews these areas and issues the picture is dynamic and what have been influential issues in the past may not be so in the future. In addition it should be noted that some issues are predictable and long-term in nature, such as

---

1 The mnemonic PEST stands for Political, Economic, Social and Technological drivers for change and is a handy way to ensure that all areas of the external environment that may affect an industry are reviewed. Similar mnemonics add L and E to stand for Legal and Environmental issues but I bundle Legal with Political and Environmental with Social issues to maintain brevity.

population and demographic issues whilst others are less predictable and fast-moving, such as a bank failure. Many issues are complex and interrelated, defying categorisation in the PEST formula. In the EU it can be seen that a social issue, such as the ageing population and pensions crisis, can become a political issue and may result in new legislation or regulation. The political significance is clear, the social feeling intense and the economic impact vital to understand.

Overall, the analysis should set the scene for understanding how and why bank strategies shift in the medium and longer terms and where and how the retail banking features described in this book gain significance. However, retail banking should not be seen from the perspective of the banks alone. Retail banking is about people – bank staff and customers, shareholders and pensioners, borrowers and lenders. Figure 1.1 provides a schematic diagram attempting to show that banks, and their people, are nested within a business framework that exists within a market that is influenced by external forces.

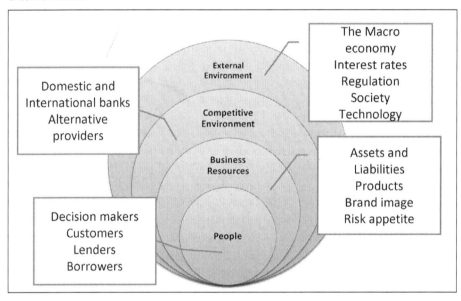

Figure 1.1: The Environment of Retail Banking

The figure simplifies the inter-relationships of environment, market and a banking business but also envelops two key ideas to be kept in mind by the reader when working through this book:

▶ The speed and complexity of change is variable
▶ Managing risk comes from within

Let me explain.

Major changes in the external environment such as regulation, economic growth or contraction, and business confidence happen reasonably gradually and are often easier to forecast. Retail banks are able to plan and manoeuvre in order to weather storms or benefit from favourable conditions but can rarely influence these drivers and can never control them. Sudden and complex change, such as the credit-crunch or an oil crisis (such as in the 1970s) take all organisations by surprise. Those surviving the storms intact have strong resources to resist the buffeting but are still at the mercy of the waves.

In the next layer of analysis, the operating or market environment, the typical retail bank is still at the mercy of decisions made by competitors and new entrants to the market but has rather more influence over its own response, its own plans and the ability of competitors to take advantage. This is recognised in Chapter 6 as many retail banks operate in markets that they dominate.

A retail bank, like any other organisation, has most influence and control over its own resources, structures, people and systems. How these are marshalled to meet the uncertainties of the external and competitive environments is the key to survival and success.

As you progress through this book consider the propensities of different banks to respond to the external factors described.

Retail banking

Retail banks are known by the products they offer to the general public. Although different banks organise their operational units in different ways, sometimes dealing with large corporate customers separately, the working definition of retail banking for the purposes of this text is the offering of banking and other financial services to individuals and Small and Medium Sized Enterprises (SMEs).

Retail banks are often prominent in their communities, with a physical presence in towns and cities. The advent of phone banking and internet banking, however, has expanded the definition. Most banks with traditional branches also boast direct phone and internet banking as additional or alternative services for customers. Some, smaller, organisations simply run internet banks, saving themselves the costs of "bricks and mortar", reducing staff requirements and even outsourcing key activities such as database maintenance, call centres and plastic card production. These can be almost "virtual" banks and although this increases competition, variety and creativity in the market, they really do nothing fundamentally different to the traditional branch-based banks.

A fuller description of key retail banking products and services is given in section B (Chapters 7 and 8) when customers and their banking relationships are reviewed. For now it is sufficient to categorise the products into two types:
1. Interest based, and
2. Non-interest based financial services

The key distinction here is the nature of the income gained by banks from these different activities. Accepting deposits and granting loans provide banks with the opportunity to gain interest income. Clearly savings interest rates will be lower than loan rates and from the difference banks must deduct their costs of operation in order to arrive at a profit. We will see in Chapter 8 that about 50% of bank incomes arise from net interest earnings.

The less risky, but also less profitable, area of income generation is the sale of financial services such as insurance, life assurance, pensions, foreign exchange, and share purchase and sale. An important part of bank income is also generated by fees charged for arranging larger loans, transmission of money and charges for unauthorised overdrafts.

Figure 1.2 summarises the "value loop" that retail banks operate. It is a "value loop" rather than a "value chain" since suppliers (those with deposits to lend to a bank) can also be customers (those who wish to borrow). The "loop" also mimics the flow of income in an economy. What is clear is that the resources that flow through the "loop" and fuel banking are twofold:

▶ Money, and
▶ Information

Retail banks collect funds from depositors in order to lend to borrowers. From each interaction the store of information about the market, the customer base and the environment is enhanced. Retail banks use the information in pursuit of their own profits – by selecting low risk borrowers and potential buyers of financial services.

The market is served by a variety of delivery channels either owned or shared by banks. Banks jostle for market position through provision of services, differentiating their offerings through brand awareness, service quality and risk management.

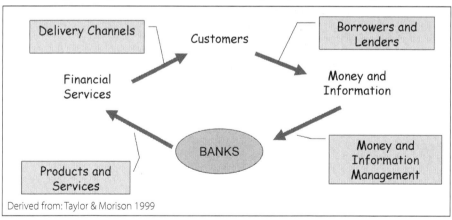

Derived from: Taylor & Morison 1999

Figure 1.2: Retail banking at work

Political and legal drivers

As we will see in section B of this text also, legislation and law-making must be reviewed constantly by banks as changes in statutes can change operational procedures, introduce new risks and, almost invariably, result in higher costs. The sources of law and regulation for retail banks are numerous and include:

- ▶ the G10 countries[2] (or at least their standing committee of bank supervisors that meets in Basel, Switzerland)
- ▶ the Central Bank/National Regulator
- ▶ The National government
- ▶ The US government, through its extra-territorial legislation (e.g. Sarbanes-Oxley Act, 2002)
- ▶ the European Parliament
- ▶ the National courts (with, of course, appeals to the International Court of Human Rights in some cases)
- ▶ International Accounting Standards

This list is not exhaustive and the key sources of law will be seen in action in various chapters of this text. However, this chapter covers only the key themes rather than the details:

Regulation

In the 2005 annual "Banana skins[3]" survey of top bankers the level and complexity of international regulation was seen as the biggest risk facing the industry. Regulation certainly increases costs as new procedures, new reporting and compliance management. This can be burdensome for smaller banks. However, it is the ever increasing march of detailed regulation of all aspects of the financial services industry, the interpretation of the rules and the impact that they have on a bank's competitive position that is of most concern. Banks are, perhaps, the most closely regulated organisations in the world but, as we will see in Chapter 5, the management of the national economy relies heavily on the banking system being stable and responsive to change.

By 2007 the biggest risk in the "Banana skins" survey was seen to be the "exotic" financial instruments that were very complex and poorly understood as well as being poorly regulated. 2008 saw bank liquidity as the top concern although this focused on the lack of market liquidity rather than the potential regulation of it.

---

2 Belgium, Canada, France, Germany, Italy, Japan, the Netherlands, Sweden, Switzerland, the United Kingdom and the United States are collectively the G10 countries. Yes, I know that there are 11 of them but the G10 name sticks. Luxembourg is an associate member – so 12.

3 The annual "Banana skins" survey is commissioned and carried out by a "thinktank" organisation known as CSFI (Centre for Study of Financial Innovation) and published in Financial World magazine.

By 2012 the CSFI were reflecting that macro-economic uncertainty and the credit risk that stemmed from it. Liquidity was also an issue but political interference and regulation had been relegated to sixth place in the table.

Regulation is seen as a necessary protection for consumers by many governments around the world. It also acts to improve consumer confidence in using financial services. Regulation ensures that consumers receive a good level of clear information about the financial products they are purchasing. Inherent in this is a warning about the risks involved. Criminal activity can also be reduced. In the past fraud and theft by so called "investment advisors" was much easier than it is today. In addition the market concentration of banking firms in many countries – see Chapter 6 – can lead to abuse of monopoly or oligopoly power. Regulation tries to ensure that the adverse effects of this situation are reduced.

The regulation of capital adequacy (in order to prevent bank failures) is dealt with in more detail in Chapter 5, together with other major areas of regulation affecting retail banks. Before 1988 national supervisory authorities such as The Bank of England in the UK oversaw the banks in their own countries. Some high profile bank failures, and the subsequent harmful effects to their home economies, caused the G10 countries to act to try to prevent this in the future. The result, known as the Basel accord, was followed by a second accord effective in 2007. The credit crunch has seen changes to Basel 2 and stronger regulation of bank liquidity in the latest adaptation of the accord.

Supervisory regulation is detailed in Chapter 6. Here it is sufficient to understand that whilst the regulatory rules (such as those issued by the Financial Conduct Authority (FCA) in the UK) are comprehensive, and often seen to be burdensome by bank staff, they are risk-based, recognising the key risks in banking and acting to ensure that individual institutions do not undertake more risk than they can manage, physically or financially. This is particularly important due to the huge web of inter-bank transactions and the increasing complexity of financial instruments such as derivatives and futures. Failure of one bank could, in theory, cause problems for others in the system and for the economy as a whole due to the knock-on or "contagion" effects. It is outside the scope of this text to discuss the particular attributes of the more complex financial instruments. More information can be found, however, in the book *Know the City 2013/14* by Chris Stoakes – see the further reading section at the end of this chapter.

Lastly we can consider, briefly The Sarbanes-Oxley Act. This US legislation was designed to restore confidence after the Enron/Worldcom corporate collapses and the question marks left over the quality of the auditing of their accounts. The legislation is extra-territorial thus affecting any UK company (including banks) seeking a listing on the US exchanges. For UK banks and financial institutions this means extra cost through having to comply with double audit standards and potential conflict with some areas of UK corporate governance. UK law and practice gives shareholders rights and voting power in meetings. By contrast US shareholders often seek court redress as they have little influence otherwise. The implications of this Act are not yet fully understood.

Taken together the instruments and bodies that combine to regulate banks in the UK have the overall aim of protecting the consumer, from unfairness, from loss due to recklessness by an individual bank, and from economic instability. These themes will be seen again in subsequent chapters.

Deregulation

Deregulation would seem to be the opposite of regulation yet this is not the case. Deregulation refers to legislation or relaxation of market based rules that remove barriers to financial services institutions engaging in different types of business. One aim of this approach is to increase competition in financial markets, giving consumers greater choice.

The 1980s were an unprecedented period of deregulation and financial liberalisation throughout the developed world. In the UK the year 1979 saw exchange controls, in place since World War 2, removed. This allowed freer capital movements between financial centres and helped London to become a global financial centre. One effect of this was to increase the number of international banks with a presence in the UK, although few of these ventured into the retail market at first.

The year 1986 was a watershed for financial services institutions in the UK. This year saw the reform of the London Stock Exchange – "Big Bang" – with the market's previously protected firms now open to competition. The banks saw a golden opportunity to buy stockbroking firms and gain a foothold in the equities markets. Some later regretted their purchases but their willingness to invest was a sure sign of the widening scope of banks and their transformation into financial conglomerates.

The ultimate picture over the last three decades is that the increased competition hoped for has not materialised in all banking markets. In retail banking this was seen in the competition authorities' response to mergers during the credit crunch. In the UK the EU rules forced RBS and Lloyds Banking Group to divest themselves of branches acquired as mergers took place. Pressures to grow, provide better returns to shareholders, achieve economies of scale and to achieve adequacy of capital in order to cover perceived risks have combined to increase merger activity and further reduce the number of institutions. Other drivers, too, have operated against the forces for de-regulation whilst some have increased competition.

Regulation is thus a mixture of international agreements, national laws, market pressures and self-control. It is a complex area to study but this brief introduction, and the follow up in forthcoming chapters provides a review of the key drivers and areas to be aware of.

Economic drivers

This section concentrates on the impact of macroeconomic conditions (economic growth, inflation etc.) on retail banking. Dealing with money and, ultimately consumer confidence, banks are particularly prone to impacts from the business cycle. Strategic decisions to expand to foreign countries or globally or simply to expand into different product areas can be seen as a product of risk-spreading. The global bank HSBC, for example, sees Europe and the USA, Asia and South America as three distinct parts of the world in which to grow. If the western economies are weak, profits will come from growth in the other two areas as they may be influenced by different economic conditions at the time. Similarly, domestic banks can expand geographically or diversify into different product areas to protect income in times of instability.

It is very clear that since the economic downturn of the early 1980s, bank profits have boomed in times of growth and have fallen in recession, largely due to bad debt write-offs. Most of this volatility relates to savings and loan part of the business and is affected by consumer incomes and their propensity to save or invest (greater when incomes are high) and to repay borrowing (lower when incomes fall). In the UK, house prices are seen as a barometer and sometimes a cause of increased propensity to borrow (especially as so many people in the UK aspire to own their own homes). This driver is not as apparent in mainland Europe where renting is more prevalent.

Banks responded to the losses of the 1980s by diversifying and increasing the proportion of fee-based services as part of their income, especially in the domestic market. They also engaged in further merger activity. Banks also made large numbers of individuals redundant and invested heavily in new technology as a way to reduce staffing costs.

The years of recession around the world have inevitably been associated with low official interest rates. Low interest rates, however, are a double-edged sword for banks. Whilst they allow for cheaper capital raising, lower interest rates offered to depositors and relatively low rates for borrowers (helping to increase customers' hunger for credit) they also store up problems for the future:

Take a moment to consider this dilemma:

With high inflation and interest rates (the two go hand in hand) a mortgage borrower may struggle to pay interest on a loan from their monthly salary. This will limit the amount borrowed in the first place, meaning that there is less capital to repay. In addition the high inflation will erode the value of the capital sum, making that easier to repay in the longer-run out of future income.

Low inflation and low interest increase the amount that can be borrowed as monthly interest is easy to pay. This means that there is a greater capital sum to repay. Inflation, however, does not erode the capital sum and so this becomes relatively more difficult to repay from future earnings.

OK the banks can always realise the security of the house to get repaid but that is not always what is intended when the loan is granted.

It has also been seen that low interest rates and margins helped to prompt the riskier elements of banking activity since these appeared to offer bigger returns. Rather than spread risk to a wider range of investors, however, banks themselves took on more and more risk to boost short-term gains.

In a similar way those relying on savings and investments and pensions backed by shares will see lower returns during times of low inflation and so more current income must be sacrificed to provide a good pension. Since few people do decide to sacrifice current income this, too, is storing up problems for the future and consumer education is vital to avoid a crisis. The fear is that many individuals will reach retirement with large loans to repay and insufficient income from pensions.

Until 2007 institutions were typically strong and profitable and most were well capitalised on accepted measures. Bank failures were rare and caused by poor management and inadequate supervision rather than a lack of capital. However, the turning consumer credit cycle became a threat. Improving incomes, rising asset prices, consumer confidence and expectations and low interest rates have combined to create a boom in consumer borrowing.

In 2013 retail banks have written off much of the bad debt accumulated in the "good" years but the suspicion remains that the write-offs have not ended. Many so-called "Zombie" companies are having loans rolled over and are paying interest only.

Thus, banks are very prone to changes in the economic cycle and we have seen a period of relative calm over the last decade followed by five years of turmoil. Bad debts can destroy profits and so geographical or product line diversification away from credit products has been seen in many retail banking operations.

Social drivers

Like all businesses banks rely on the demand created by individuals and industry to generate income and profit. Clearly where population and entrepreneurial activity increase banks can grow and, in general terms, retail banks have benefited from this over the years. Changes in our demographics and social norms, however, ensure that banks need to maintain constant vigilance to provide the products and services that people actually want to buy.

Some key trends over recent years have been:
▶ The ageing population
▶ A changing ethnic mix

▶ Increasing expectations
▶ Declining institutional trust
▶ Greater financial self-reliance
▶ Greater awareness of environmental and ethical issues

All of these combine to provide fairly predictable social drivers that banks need to respond to. The following section summarises some of the key trends mentioned above.

Across Europe and the UK it is clear (with plenty of statistics available) that birth rates are falling, young people are staying in full-time education for longer and old people are living longer. This squeezes the number of people in the workforce and leads to a demand for inward immigration, a change in traditional family roles as more and more women join the workforce to fill job gaps and the employment of individuals until well past their retirement age.

Most of this seems good news but as with the low inflation mentioned above it can store up problems for the future and this is already being recognised by pension providers in particular.

The point about social change is that banks must respond in the short term and the longer term to these changes. The provision of pensions is a particular problem as state pensions rely on current taxation from workers to fund payments to retirees. With more retired people and fewer workers a "black hole" in the national finances emerges. People are being encouraged, therefore, to provide more for their own retirement and not to rely solely on the state. Banks respond to this by offering products that can make this additional saving possible.

Managed immigration to help swell the workforce (and the impact of enlarging the EU to allow freedom of movement of European workers) has also led to a diverse and ethnically mixed society. Whilst many celebrate the diversity banks are aware that their financial needs must be met and that traditional banking systems and products may not be the solution. In some cultures families, rather than banks, are the first resort for credit and extended families can obviate the need for substantial pension provision.

One interesting example of social change in the UK is the provision of "Islamic[4]" finance by mainstream banks. In short, traditional planning assumptions for a domestic population must be amended.

Other social trends, some a by-product of increasing economic prosperity and government policies through the years, are raising expectations and increased financial self-reliance. Again, banks must be aware of attitude changes and can see that the

---

4 Islamic finance is a generic term to describe the types of financial products acceptable to Sharia law for the Muslim religion. Under Sharia law the charging and payment of interest is forbidden. Thus many traditional banking products would be shunned by followers of this law. Islamic finance constructs financing deals so that rewards are available to the lender but no interest is charged.

boom in consumer credit owes as much to the availability of credit as to the desire to own the nicest house, the newest car, the latest electronic gadgets and go on exotic holidays, formerly the preserve of the super-rich. Individual expectations have grown as educational standards have improved and mass media has shown us the possibilities.

At the same time, however, less state support has meant greater self reliance. Three areas worth mentioning here are pensions (see above), home ownership and student loans. All of these create increased demand for higher paid jobs and these, in turn, rely on an ever-growing economy. Expectations are high but the fear is that some of these will be unmet and the backlash will damage the inherent trust in government (perhaps too late?) and banking institutions. Already the large numbers of bankruptcies in the UK indicate that more people are willing to find an alternative to repaying credit in full. Interestingly banks have spent years closing branches, reducing staff and pushing customers away by installing remote banking facilities. It is easier to trust somebody you know and for more and more customers their "bank manager" is an unknown figure.

Finally, in this section, banks must reflect changing social attitudes to the environment and to ethical behaviour. As global institutions many banks play a key role in the financing of civil construction, house-building and industrialisation. Increasingly shareholders, customers, staff and governments require environmental audits of projects so that the benefits of projects can be weighed against both economic and environmental costs. Many banks now publish "corporate responsibility" reports, sharing information about these issues as they recognise the desire of their stakeholders to hold them to account.

This can only be a very "broad brush" approach to social drivers in the banking industry but it does serve to illustrate that banks cannot be static in their views or offerings and that the banks that innovate, reflecting changing social trends, may be the survivors in the future, rather than those that are overtaken by events.

One key feature of the credit-crunch has been the loss of trust in financial institutions – and trust is central to the smooth running of a credit creating banking system. Banks will have to work hard to regain the trust of depositors in the future.

Technological drivers

This section can do no more than scratch the surface of the use of technology by retail banks. It is not intended to be an exhaustive list of technological innovation although some technologies will be introduced in later chapters as they have become key delivery mechanisms for banks. Rather, I want to illustrate the use of technology and its implications by reference to the core competencies of banks including:

- Information Advantages
- Risk Analysis Expertise

▶ Monitoring of Borrowers
▶ Broking Potential
▶ Delivery Capacity

According to the title of a 2005 history of retail banking "Other people's money" is what banking is all about. Chapter 2 of this text expands on this idea but it should be remembered that banks do not lend their own funds; rather they are intermediaries between lenders and borrowers, having honed the core competencies listed above to ensure that the most efficient and profitable use is made of other people's money.

Technology and computerisation has accelerated in complexity, reliability and availability over the last 60 years. From the first modern computers in the 1940s (machines that could fill an entire office block) to today's smartphones and tablets banks have tried to harness the benefits of technology to support core functions.

Banks gather and store large amounts of information about us including information on our jobs, homes, spending, credit and repayment records. They know when and where we spend our money and can forecast when we may need particular banking services. The information is most obviously used in analysing the creditworthiness of customers and judging the credit risk inherent in lending proposals. Additionally banks are in a unique position to monitor the repayment of loans and forecast when problems can arise. This can prompt them to take action to remedy a situation or re-negotiate a loan so that repayment is assured.

Banks also communicate worldwide via computers, allowing access to world markets to their clients. Whilst most domestic clients will not require such wide-reaching services the same basic technology is used to make customer information available at any branch of the bank (previously a customer had to attend their own branch to transact business) or any internet terminal. Such communication power allows banks to interact with each other, provide swifter settlement of inter-bank debts and give access to stock exchange, insurance, investment and currency exchange services.

Banks' own costs can also be affected by technology. In the short run investment in computing power is expensive both in financial terms and possibly in reputational terms if it does not work as expected. A number of banks have suffered bad publicity and, perhaps, a loss of trust, when internet banking systems have revealed private account information to those it was not intended for. This, however, is simply a modern incarnation of the problem of maintaining secrecy and security that has always existed.

Investment in systems also brings longer-term cost benefits. Estimated costs of internet transactions are a small percentage of the cost of branch-based ones. Electronic payment systems, such as debit cards, are far cheaper than cheques. This is due not only to the lower fixed costs of the systems but also because it allows banks to reduce staff numbers or at least release staff to sell products to customers rather than engage in un-remunerative administrative processing work. Technology also allows telephone call centres to be located in low-wage parts of the world such as India but this too can have drawbacks for customer relationships.

I end this section with a note of warning, however. Technology will not ever completely replace the need for human interaction, especially where complex financial products are concerned. Banks embrace improvements in technology as these can reduce costs and maximise flexibility and reach but they will always have to employ people. Additionally banking technology is available to any firm wishing to invest and so non-banking institutions have begun to enter the retail banking market, concentrating on smaller, profitable areas of the business rather than the whole range of products traditionally offered.

So, what is it all about?

This is a central question that has driven me to write this book and to be engaged in teaching about banking all over the world. I can imagine a world without computers, I can imagine a world with different national and international boundaries, different governments, different social values and different tastes and preferences – but I cannot imagine a world (for very long) without the key ingredients of banking – money and people. Where these exist together banks will emerge to service their needs and to profit in so doing.

This book attempts to explain in reasonably simple terms a very complex global industry. Its detailed interactions often defy basic explanation but the fact that they affect all of our lives is certain.

I hope that by reading this book you will learn just how retail banks work, what they do and how and why they do it.

Summary

This chapter has covered:
- ▶ Current and pervasive trends in the retail banking environment.
- ▶ Political and legal drivers for change.
- ▶ Economic conditions and their general effect on banking.
- ▶ Social and technological issues driving strategies in retail banking.
- ▶ The outline of this book.

Further Reading

Lascelles D, (2005), *Other People's Money: The Revolution in High Street Banking*, London, Institute of Financial Services, ISBN: 1845163516

Stoakes C, (2013), *Know the City*, 2013/14 edn., Christopher Stoakes Ltd.

CHAPTER 2

What is Retail Banking?

Objectives

After studying this chapter you should be able to:
- ▶ Describe the key functions of different types of bank
- ▶ Distinguish between Commercial banking and Investment banking
- ▶ List the activities undertaken by a "Universal" bank
- ▶ Explain the key banking function of Intermediation
- ▶ Link the features of Intermediation with some of the practical measures that banks take (expanded in later chapters).
- ▶ Explain the benefits of Intermediation
- ▶ Compare Intermediation and Disintermediation
- ▶ Describe how banks create credit

Introduction

The organisations that we typically think of as banks are far more than just that; they are financial conglomerates undertaking a wide range of activities. In this text we are interested in banking, the original meaning of the word, and even more narrowly – retail banking – the provision of banking services to individuals and companies.

This chapter begins with a brief review of the different types of "banking" and the constituent parts of the "Universal" or conglomerate bank in order to distinguish between them and to introduce some of the seemingly confusing terminology in this area. Although the distinctions regarding functions are made clear large banks go to great lengths to ensure that corporate customers, in particular, do not see the joins (or gaps) between the different parts of the bank. They prefer to present an integrated whole, using one brand image (the HSBC logo is used globally) often "fronted" by a relationship manager who manages the relationship and gains access, on behalf of the customer, to the different parts of the bank services.

Regulatory frameworks, however, can force artificial "walls" between different parts of a universal bank. Chapter 5 on bank regulation illustrates how this separation impacts on bank strategy.

The chapter goes on to review some of the key concepts in banking that attempt to answer the question – "What is it that retail banks actually do?" The concept of intermediation will be explored and some of the risks associated with money and credit will be explained. The chapter continues with an illustration of how the banking system creates credit. The chapter introduces Chapter 3's dissection of a typical bank balance sheet when additional concepts of interest rate risk and liquidity risk are discussed.

Banks can make multibillion pound profits annually due to their size, the expertise of their staff and their command of banking technologies. Whilst reading this chapter it may be instructive to ask yourself – "If banks did not exist, would they be invented?" Decide for yourself whether banks perform a useful function for the economy.......

Types of banking

Over the past 100 years, where regulatory pressures, deregulation and competition have allowed, banks around the world have grown in size not only through expansion but also through mergers and joint ventures.

Expansion, allowing access to larger capital and deposit resources, can often be linked back to regulatory capital requirements. The advance of technology, economies of scale and scope also present themselves as drivers for consolidation. UK banking provides an illustration of this with a brief history illustrated in Figure 2.1.

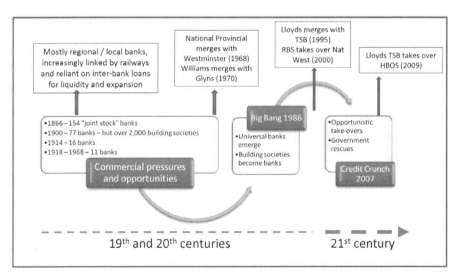

Figure 2.1: A timeline of UK bank consolidation

Consolidation and merger have occurred not only geographically and horizontally (banks joining with similar banks) but between the different types of banks. As seen in Chapter 1 this was made possible by deregulation in the 1980s. The result is a small number of global universal banks – many of which have retail banking functions in numerous territories.

Figure 2.2 shows the constituent parts of a universal bank. In reality the boundaries between activities are not as clear as this:

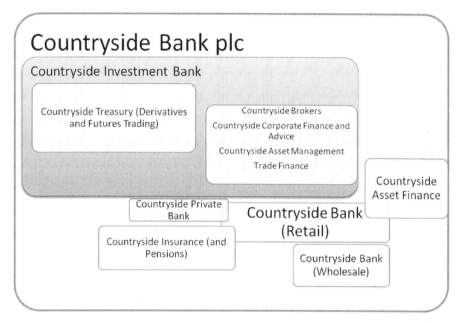

Figure 2.2: The constituent parts of a universal bank

Commercial banking

Commercial banking is the traditional role of the banker as it relates to the taking of deposits and granting of loans. Commercial banking activity is split into two types:

Retail banking and

Wholesale banking.

The key differentiation between these is that retail banks borrow from and lend to members of the public and companies whilst wholesale banks deal with other banks and with governments (national and overseas). Note the terminology here: in a legal sense banks borrow funds from depositors. The money deposited belongs to the bank with the normal condition that it is returned to the depositor on demand (immediately) or on the expiry of a notice period (seven days is common). Actually, in practice, banks allow depositors to withdraw funds on demand, even from "time" deposits but charge a penalty by deducting the interest for the notice period. We will see in Chapter 4 that customer deposits are liabilities in bank balance sheets and loans are assets.

Just like individuals, banks themselves, and governments need to deposit funds and to borrow from other banks to maintain liquidity. If a bank only lends out the funds deposited by its own customers it may miss the opportunity to expand its lending portfolio due to a lack of liquidity. If it lends out funds needed to repay deposits it can run out of money. Any rumour that a bank cannot repay its depositors can cause other depositors to demand their money back. The bank suffers what is called a "run on the bank", normally fatal for the bank and possibly for the whole banking system. *The Run on the Rock*, the government's investigation into the failure of Northern Rock plc in 2007, highlights the "run" seen and compares it with the 1866 "run" on Overend Gurney and Co., the last UK bank to suffer in this way.….until 2007.

Also the situation can arise that a bank has funds deposited that it does not need to lend to customers. If it keeps these in cash the deposits earn nothing and so a bank can lend the excess funds to other banks either overnight or for a longer period and make a profit from its "idle" balances.

Wholesale banking activities, therefore, ensure that any liquidity gap that the bank may estimate or calculate, on a daily basis, is covered by borrowing from other banks and any surplus funds are invested by depositing them with (lending them to) other banks or to the government. For these activities banks use their own interest rate – LIBOR – the London Inter-Bank Offered Rate. This is the key to understanding how government monetary policy is effected through the banking system. We will explore this in more detail in Chapter 4.

In providing this central function of intermediation (especially between retail customers) banks have developed efficient and secure payment systems.

Investment banking

Investment banks are a US creation, brought about by the Glass-Steagall[5] Act of the 1930s. Under this law the two aspects of banking – Commercial and Investment could not be combined in one institution. Although the legislation has now been repealed its legacy in the US was that different banks with similar names emerged, only re-combining under universal bank banners. This legislation did not have an impact on purely UK banks as the US legislation was not extra-territorial. In addition the UK had a tradition of separation of these functions. In the UK investment banks were called Merchant

---

5 Glass-Steagall was passed as a reaction to numerous bank failures in the Wall Street Crash of 1929 and the Great Depression of the 1930s. It separated the savings and loan activities of banks from their "investment" activities as so many banks had used deposits to buy shares that then lost value in the Crash. Commercial pressures blurred this distinction in the latter half of the 20th century (universal banks) and the Act was finally repealed in 1999. Its legacy, however, was that separate banks emerged (e.g JP Morgan Chase and Morgan Stanley).

banks. Merchant banks take their name from their original activity of providing trade finance. In Figure 2.2 (above) Trade Finance can be part of the commercial bank or the investment bank – there are no hard and fast rules.

So what is investment banking? Again, there are no rules to determine the functions undertaken by an investment bank. Much investment banking activity is focused on trading with clients, the bank acting as an agent. However, some activity can be for the bank's "own account", where the bank actively buys and sells securities and bonds, derivatives and futures in order to achieve profits – so called proprietary trading. In a traditional investment bank there are three key activities:

- Underwriting of bond and share issues
- Purchase and sale of issued (second-hand) securities
- Processing of futures, swaps etc. on behalf of clients.
- To these functions, carried out on behalf of clients, must be added similar activities where the bank trades for its own account – engaging in proprietary trading and risking the bank's capital in so doing.

Underwriting often follows the provision of advice to corporate customers wishing to raise finance by issuing shares to the public or issuing bonds (loan notes) to the public. The reasons that some companies prefer to raise finance in this way are numerous and outside the scope of this text but they have to do with the fact that it is cheaper than borrowing from a commercial bank. Underwriting is the mechanism whereby the Investment bank agrees to buy or fund the share or bond issue, guaranteeing that the company obtains the funding it seeks. In turn the investment bank will have made arrangements for other institutions to buy some or all of that issue, otherwise the bank can be left with a large block of shares or bonds that nobody wants. Without demand for the securities these will reduce in value and cause the bank to lose money. Clearly successful underwriting needs an excellent understanding of the markets.

With underwriting, therefore banks can use some of their own capital if they end up owning any of the shares or bonds although this is not their primary motive. Once issued, the securities can be traded and this is the second function mentioned above. In buying and selling shares and bonds banks either work on behalf of their clients, providing advice and execution of deals, or they can trade on their own account. This activity also extends to asset management, where portfolios of shares and investments are managed on behalf of clients (private banks[6] are small investment banks that typically look after a small number of super-rich clients).

Deployment of risk mitigation tolls for clients, for a fee, has been a growing part of investment banking. It is far beyond the scope of an introductory text to cover the

---

6 Private banks exist in the UK but are more prevalent in "tax havens" such as Jersey, Guernsey, The Isle of Man, Liechtenstein, San Marino, Singapore and Switzerland – the largest private bank in the world is UBS (Union Bank of Switzerland).

economics of derivatives, futures and swaps but this is dealt with in some detail by Chris Stoakes in his excellent book *Know the City*.

Derivatives, "exotic" securities and "casino banking" are not bad *per se* but some of the assumptions about risk spreading and the underlying value of assets should have been better understood by traders.

Proprietary trading must also be well understood and regulated as the currency of investment banking is information as well as money and banks must take great care not to profit from their own clients' confidences.

Bankassurance

This term is of interest to a study of retail banking because it describes those banks that have purchased or created insurance companies and pension funds as part of their "universal" status. Having an in-house insurance company does allow for cross-selling within the retail bank network. This provides an additional benefit to the profits that can be generated through this activity generally. In addition the main source of funds for pensions and insurers to invest in shares and bonds come from retail and wholesale banking activities. Since insurance companies and pension fund managers undertake very similar activities to the fund managers and asset managers in a bank's investment banking arm there can be considerable synergies in becoming a bankassurer. It is enough, for the purposes of this text, to leave the discussion of bankassurance there.

To conclude this section of Chapter 2 it does seem fairly easy to distinguish between the different types of banking by looking at activities, customers or products. In practice there are large differences between the different types of banking, different histories of the companies within the same bank, different skills required from staff and different rewards[7] available. There are also huge similarities in the concepts underlying all types of banking and the next section covers some of these major theoretical areas.

Key banking concepts

The two key banking concepts that are covered in this section are those of iIntermediation, the position of banks as "middlemen" between those with money to lend and those wishing to borrow, and the creation of credit. The creation of credit by banks, like the payments system is a by-product of intermediation. In later chapters some of the ideas and themes discussed here will be further expanded.

---

[7] The particular skills and competencies of good investment banking managers can attract rewards through high salaries and even higher bonus payments. In comparison the lower salaries offered in commercial banking look derisory. However, aspiring investment managers must realise that the risks associated with high rewards are higher, the chance of failure greater (often associated with market trends) and the jobs less long-term.

Intermediation and credit creation rely on the legal and practical principle that, once deposited, a bank can use the funds at its own discretion subject to the need to repay them to the borrower on demand. The skill of the retail banker is to balance the needs of the lenders and borrowers it has as customers and to make a profit for its shareholders in doing so.

The more modern concept of Disintermediation – where individuals and firms lend and borrow without doing so via a traditional bank is also worth consideration.

Intermediation

The concept of banking intermediation recognizes that there are two types of player (individuals, governments, companies, banks) in the financial system:
- ▷ Surplus units and
- ▷ Deficit units

We will call these "units" Lenders and Borrowers.

Of course those with surpluses of money have no obligation to lend them. For generations individuals have put their money under their beds or have buried it in their gardens. Of course this has dangers both physical (theft or destruction) and economic through inflation or devaluation of a currency.

However to make best use of the money they have available to lend, a lender needs to seek out a borrower or borrowers. The levels of interest rates will have a bearing on where funds are deposited. In the low interest rate conditions seen in the US, UK, EU and for even longer, in Japan, direct deposits from savers can reduce as they seek higher returns (and higher risk) in alternative investments.

There are FOUR main ways that lenders and borrowers interact as illustrated in Figure 2.3:

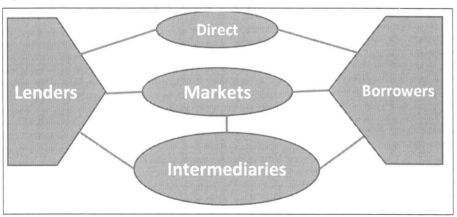

Figure 2.3: Borrowers and lenders

1. Direct dealing with each other (financial disintermediation).
2. Dealing via the market (Bond Market, Currency Market, Money Market)
3. Dealing via an intermediary (Bank or Building Society)
4. Intermediaries dealing through the markets with securitisation of loans.

For the vast majority of the population only option 3 above is realistic but for large companies direct dealing is becoming more prevalent. Disintermediation was initially seen as a threat to banks but it undermines only a traditional role, banks can offer disintermediation services for their corporate clients, understanding that this is now a real option for them. Investment banks will cater for those companies wishing to deal via the markets as seen above.

Disintermediation

Low and volatile returns from traditional investments, together with communication via the internet, have made disintermediation available to individuals – both as consumers and small businesses. Peer-to-Peer (P2P) lending was born in the USA and is now available in Western Europe. Sites such as Zopa (personal deposits and loans), ThinCats (small business secured loans) and Funding Circle (business loans) attract lenders who choose the level of risk they wish to assume, and borrowers who bid for loans.

The model for many P2P sites, which promises better returns to lenders and better deals for borrowers than traditional banks, is akin to that of a dating website. For a commission or "finder's fee" the site vets potential borrowers by performing a credit check or a more thorough investigation for business loans and distributes funds.

Lenders spread risk by lending limited amounts to a range of borrowers and can often decide the level of interest they require. Borrowers limit costs by stipulating the rates they are willing to pay.

The benefits of intermediation

Financial intermediation, however, remains the norm for most customers as they gain considerable benefits through the use of banks. These benefits or qualities can be summarized as follows:
- MATURITY TRANSFORMATION
- ASSET TRANSFORMATION (AGGREGATION)
- RISK TRANSFORMATION
- GEOGRAPHICAL LOCATION

M.A.R.G. may not be the snappiest abbreviation but it does provide a method of remembering the four key attributes of intermediation.

Maturity transformation refers to banks offering liquidity to customers. Liquidity means having money available quickly either by withdrawing deposits or being granted a loan that is repaid over time. Customer needs do not coincide. Typically depositors want their funds available on demand, so that funds can be withdrawn at any time. Current accounts are "on demand" and whilst many savings accounts are "time deposits" banks often allow withdrawal on demand.

Borrowers, however, wish to repay loans at the latest possible date. Companies repay loans out of profits and these may take years to materialize after an investment is made. Mortgage loans are repaid from monthly income over periods of 25 or 30 years. By pooling funds (much as insurance companies and pension funds do as they too are intermediaries) banks achieve a balance so that they hold just enough cash to satisfy the immediate withdrawals of their customers whilst retaining enough to lend to borrowers.

This feature of intermediation is the concept behind the creation of credit by banks and this will be dealt with later in this chapter. Using their vast experience and knowledge banks are able to estimate, on a daily basis, how much liquidity their customers require. For example, as the holiday season or Christmas approaches savings are withdrawn to meet increased expenses.

As mentioned above a by-product of financial intermediation is the maintenance of a payments or clearing system so that customers may make withdrawals quickly and conveniently. Without a method of withdrawal few customers would commit their savings to a bank.

The pooling of funds on the scale achieved by banks is known as **asset transformation or aggregation**. Depositors' funds, added together, can be invested in a wider and more diversified way than a depositor could achieve alone. This helps to reduce risk for the depositor. This also helps to reduce potential returns as interest rates offered on current accounts or "demand" deposits are very low.

So, we can see that the benefits of intermediation are linked closely with one another. **Risk transformation** is the third feature. This relies not only on the banks' ability to garner deposit funds and enjoy the benefits of pooling but also on bank lending expertise. Banks may enjoy economies of scale and lower unit costs through efficiencies in payments systems and organizational systems. They also enjoy economies of scope in the use of the information they garner about individual customers.

By using a bank as an intermediary the risk of losing funds that have been deposited is lessened as the bank has considerable expertise in assessing creditworthiness, monitoring repayment of loans and pursuing "bad" debts if the borrower fails to repay. Banks also hold sufficient *capital* (their own funds) to cover likely losses and so depositors should never fear that their money will be lost – in theory at least! All of these issues are expanded upon in later chapters.

The final benefit of intermediation is that of **geographical location**. UK banks have invested heavily in branch networks (19th century), amalgamations and mergers (19th and 20th centuries) and the internet (20th century). A primary aim of achieving good geographical and virtual coverage is that it is easier for depositors to both deposit and withdraw funds. When we look at the history of UK banking in Chapter 3 we will note that in 17th century Cornwall (for example) depositors' funds would most likely be lent to individuals or businesses in Cornwall. This would severely limit the returns available and would operate at a higher risk level – giving rise to pressures for merger that continues to this day.

Comparing intermediation and P2P lenders

On the face of it the P2P sites offer a service just like a traditional bank. Look closer, however, and the better returns for lenders and lower costs for borrowers are "paid" for in other ways.

If we take the four key benefits of intermediation we can see that P2P sites certainly offer Asset Transformation/Aggregation as many lenders combine to make a loan to a borrower. Geographical location is also covered through the availability of the internet and use of electronic payments.

Maturity and Risk Transformation, however, are not comparable. P2P sites absorb none of the risks associated with repayment of loans. Lenders will lose a proportion of their capital over time unless they are very lucky. If a lender wishes to withdraw their loan the site may restrict this or offer an auction facility where others can bid for the loan obligations – this may result in the original lender accepting less than the face value of the loan ("taking a haircut").

Trust

One final question about intermediation that banks must appreciate is: How do banks attract lenders?

Keen observers will note that banks market their brand image very well and are amongst the most frequent TV advertisers and sport sponsors. They also offer interest to depositors (lenders) but as the rates offered by different banks are very similar most of the time this can account for only some of their attraction. A unique feature of banks, however, is the degree of confidence and trust placed in them by customers. This is a feature that banks rely on heavily as, unlike a manufacturer, there is no physical "product" to show or feel to help to generate confidence.

Thus, intermediation gives rise to a need for banks to show that they are trustworthy, secure, prudent and expert at their trade. Over the many years of banking activity this has given rise to the bankers' duty of secrecy, the building of visibly strong branches with wrought iron and marble columns to denote solidity in Victorian times and the focus on brand image in current times. Also showing good credit judgement and suffering few losses due to non-repayment of loans boosts confidence in a bank. Ironically making billions of pounds in profits can cause public outcry, yet the level of profit is often the product of the prudence, confidence and trust that we demand of our banks.

Following the credit-crunch retail banks are at the forefront of re-building public trust in the banking system. Bankers' bonuses, bank profits, access to house mortgage and SME finance have all been battlegrounds in the years since 2007. Particular blows have also come from a series of mis-selling crises. In the 1990s Private Pensions and Endowment policies were mis-sold to millions. The credit crunch highlighted the ease with which credit was available, especially in the UK and US markets. More recently Payment Protection Insurance (PPI) which, in many cases, was inappropriate to the needs of the borrower has resulted in £billions in compensation being paid. Identity Theft Insurance is yet another inappropriate product sold to many but where the benefits did not exceed the statutory protection afforded.

Financial losses and compensation suffered by banks in recent years are summarised at Figure 2.4:

Figure 2.4: Banking losses and compensation (2010 – 2013)

NATURE OF SCANDAL	COUNTRIES INVOLVED	LOSSES IN £ BILLIONS
Payment Protection Insurance mis-selling	UK	£15 bn.
Interest Rate Swaps mis-selling	UK	£2 bn.
Identity Theft Insurance	UK	£1.3 bn.
LIBOR "rigging"	UK, US and Europe	£2 bn. and counting
Money Laundering	UK, US and Europe	£2.2 bn.

Although the public outcry over inappropriate selling of interest rate swaps to unsophisticated small businesses and the "fixing" of LIBOR by a small number of banks has been subdued, each series of events damages the trust and esteem of banks. Perhaps the most successful bank emerging from the credit-crunch will not only be profitable (again) but also trusted by the borrowing and lending public. It may take more than clever advertising to achieve, however.

The creation of credit

A final feature of intermediation that is not obvious from the description of the benefits of this function is the creation of credit, i.e. allowing borrowers to borrow more than is actually deposited with the bank!. The principles of credit creation are applicable to all banks. In the real world some banks will be "surplus units" and some "deficit units" as far as their transactions with retail customers are concerned. It is then that they must lend to or borrow from other banks or the government to maximize profits and maintain liquidity.

In the past the early bankers (goldsmiths) came into being as traders found it more convenient and safe to deposit gold with a trusted person than to keep it on their own premises. The goldsmiths issued "notes" or IOUs to show how much gold had been deposited and, later, began to lend the gold which they had received from their customers, because not all their notes promising return of the gold would be presented at any one time.

Credit creation relies on a number of theoretical and practical assumptions relating to intermediation:

▶ There are incentives for depositors to leave funds with banks

▶ Not all deposits are required for withdrawal on demand

▶ Regulators may stipulate a "liquidity ratio" – a ratio of cash or liquid assets available to meet depositors' demands for withdrawals

▶ Regulators may also stipulate a capital ratio – a ratio that limits the amount of lending based on the equity of a bank (see Chapter 5 also)

▶ Not all loans will return to the bank/banking system as new deposits.

A summary of a banker's initial accounts might look like this:

RIVERSIDE BANK PTE LTD - BALANCE SHEET#1			
	$000		$000
Liabilities		Assets	
Customer Deposits	5,000	Cash	5,000
Loans from banks	0	Loans to banks	2,000
Corporate Bonds	4,000	Govt. Bonds	2,000
		Loans to customers	0
Equity / Reserves	1,000	Physical assets	1,000
	10,000		10,000

A further assumption is that banks aim to make profits and they do this through interest margins and fees based on payment products and non-interest products such as insurance. Chapter 8 details the various interest and non-interest products commonly available through retail banks.

So, for Riverside Bank Pte Ltd, based in Singapore, to make profits it will need to make loans to customers, subject to the liquidity and capital ratio constraints noted above. Let's assume that Riverside Bank chooses to retain $1million in cash (a 20% ratio to deposits) and to lend $4million. The result would look like this:

RIVERSIDE BANK PTE LTD – BALANCE SHEET#2			
	$000		$000
Liabilities		Assets	
Customer Deposits	5,000	Cash	1,000
Loans from banks	0	Loans to banks	2,000
Corporate Bonds	4,000	Govt. Bonds	2,000
		Loans to customers	4,000
Equity / Reserves	1,000	Physical assets	1,000
	10,000		10,000

Most of the lending will return to the banks, with only a fraction being held elsewhere in cash – perhaps in people's mattresses! – or being paid to the government, e.g. in tax or to people overseas. If we assume that $2m of the $4m lent is re-deposited by those who have sold the borrowers' houses or cars or business assets then the result becomes:

RIVERSIDE BANK PTE LTD - BALANCE SHEET#3			
	$000		$000
Liabilities		Assets	
Customer Deposits	7,000	Cash	3,000
Loans from banks	0	Loans to banks	2,000
Corporate Bonds	4,000	Govt. Bonds	2,000
		Loans to customers	4,000
Equity / Reserves	1,000	Physical assets	1,000
	12,000		12,000

The Balance Sheet footings have grown to $12m through the lending activity of the bank. With fees and interest margin income the bank should be profitable as long as loans are repaid. These profits will build up reserves in order that the capital ratio requirement can be met as loans expand.

Our final look at the Riverside Bank Balance Sheet shows the 20% liquidity ratio being retained as further loans are made based on re-deposits:

RIVERSIDE BANK PTE LTD – BALANCE SHEET#4			
	$000		$000
Liabilities		Assets	
Customer Deposits	7,000	Cash	1,400
Loans from banks	0	Loans to banks	2,000
Corporate Bonds	4,000	Govt. Bonds	2,000
		Loans to customers	5,600
Equity / Reserves	1,000	Physical assets	1,000
	12,000		12,000

Clearly the bank could meet demand for loans through other means too – by issuing more debt or equity or simply by borrowing money on the inter-bank markets, attracting deposits from other banks and institutions – the permutations are endless.

In the next chapter we see that it is not as simple as this. Different risks emerge as banks create credit, finance loan assets and compete in a dynamic economic environment.

Summary

This chapter has covered:
- Different types of banking activity
- The composition of a "universal" bank
- The key institutions in the UK retail banking market
- The concepts of intermediation and disintermediation
- The creation of credit by banks

Further reading and useful web links

Molyneux P and Goacher D, (2005) *The Monetary and Financial System* 6th edn., Global Professional Publishing.

Stoakes C, (2013), *Know the City*-2013/14, Christopher Stoakes Ltd.

Treasury Committee, (2008), *The Run on the Rock*, Vol 1, The Stationery Office.

The LIBOR scandal explained, http://www.accountingdegree.net/members/libor.php

CHAPTER 3

How Do Retail Banks Work?

Objectives

After studying this chapter you should be able to:

- ▶ Describe the key elements found in a bank balance sheet
- ▶ Explain the differences between different types of asset and liability
- ▶ Outline the key factors that impact on retail bank profitability
- ▶ Explain the key components of interest rates
- ▶ Link retail bank management to general economic and regulatory issues

Introduction

This chapter looks at the business of banking from an accounting perspective, reviews the need for liquidity, sources of profit and the treatment of assets and liabilities. The term nature of deposits and loans is addressed so that bank balance sheets can be "read" as a description of banking activity. Chapter 2 is expanded on here as liquidity and interest rate risk are discussed in more detail and the important interactions with the inter-bank market recognised more fully.

The chapter provides a foundation for the two final chapters in section A of this text as it attempts to put into perspective the various activities of the bank as an intermediary, the main factors affecting profit and loss and some of the key external issues and concepts that guide bank decisions.

A typical bank balance sheet

Figures 3.1 and 3.3 combine to provide a typical balance sheet, a snapshot of a universal bank's assets and liabilities, at 31 December (the typical year end). The balancing figure, as with every balance sheet, is the bank's own capital and it is this that will receive particular scrutiny in Chapter 6 when bank regulation is discussed.

The figures are followed by brief explanations of each type of asset and liability but provide a poor representation of the dynamic nature of asset and liability management on a day-to-day basis. The balance sheet can also be used to illustrate two key risks that banks manage:

▶ Liquidity risk, and
▶ Interest rate risk

Whilst serving the needs of their customers, meeting their obligations to other banks these institutions must also make a profit for their shareholders. The fact that many banks do this successfully, posting £billions in profits each year, is testimony to their expertise in these areas.

Figure 3.1: Assets in a Typical Bank Balance Sheet

ASSETS	£M	% OF TOTAL ASSETS
Cash & balances at central banks	1,717	0.4
Items in course of collection	3,155	0.7
Treasury & other bills	7,842	1.8
Loans and advances to banks	67,471	15.1
Loans and advances to customers	224,359	50.2
Debt securities	100,122	22.4
Equity shares	5,164	1.2
Joint ventures	454	0.1
Intangibles - Goodwill	3,867	0.9
Fixed assets	1,572	0.4
Other assets	23,366	5.2
Retail life funds	7,642	1.7
TOTAL ASSETS	446,731	

Assets

A bank's **assets** are the source of its income and profits. Clearly most banks will choose to invest in the highest quality and highest return assets available but there is also a need to maintain stability, adopt a portfolio approach, to spread risk, and to conform to capital adequacy and reserve asset ratios.

The assets shown above are:

Cash and balances at central banks

This includes notes and coins in tills and ATMs. Holding cash is expensive and earns nothing so banks want to keep this to a minimum. This also includes cash deposits at the Central Bank which earn no interest but must be maintained to allow clearing transactions and any special deposits[8].

Items in the course of collection

There is a corresponding entry under Liabilities. This is the inevitable result of operating a clearing system[9]. Within the clearing cycle these funds will be paid to the bank by those banks whose customers' cheques and payments have been collected. Since the balance sheet is struck at 31 December this will be inflated by the fact that the clearing system halts at weekends and on bank/national holidays.

Treasury bills and other eligible bills

These are 91-day bills either guaranteed at the highest commercial level (a bank) or by local authorities or the central bank. Each bill represents a short-term loan to the issuer. Accordingly the interest rate charged cannot be much different to the market rate.

Loans and advances to banks

These are largely short-term loans to other banks in the financial system and to overseas banks. Loans to discount houses[10] are included. Again, interest rates are at very low margins above market rates.

Loans and advances to customers

These include long-term and short-term loans to corporate and personal customers. Mortgages, personal loans and overdrafts are counted here. Some lending is secured and some unsecured. At over 50% of all assets these are amongst the riskiest but most profitable assets held.

In traditional retail banking the bank holds the loan asset on its own balance sheet until maturity. In the "originate to distribute" model used, for example, by Northern Rock, loans would be agreed and the corresponding liability "securitised" via an investment

---

8 Special deposits are no longer used by the Bank of England to control money supply and bank liquidity as it uses market interest rates and market intervention to do this now. In the past banks were obliged to maintain special deposits with the Bank, thus restricting the amount that they could lend

9 The UK clearing system for cheques and electronic payments is described in Chapter 10. It is a unique feature of UK banking that some banks (the clearers) own and run the clearing system as a private venture. In other European countries and in the U.S. this function is undertaken by the central bank (The Federal Reserve in the U.S. or by the government (Giro) in Europe.

10 Discount houses are specialist intermediaries dealing almost exclusively in high quality Bills of Exchange, typically generated from trading transactions of large, creditworthy clients. A discount house will lend cash on the Bill, discounting this at a rate of interest, for the period to maturity of the Bill. When the Bill is paid the discount house is repaid

vehicle – Northern Rock used Lehman Brothers. Other banks' assets were also the target of "securitisation" leading up to the credit crunch of 2007/08. A package of good quality house mortgage loans, or credit card contracts, could be bundled up by the lender and sold to an investor. The lender would receive cash that it could use to lend to new clients. The demand for securitised loans by investors, however, could lead to lower quality loans being agreed – so called "sub-prime" mortgages. The 2008 Treasury Committee report *The run on the Rock* details the events leading up to Northern Rock's failure and discusses a number of these features.

Debt securities

Longer term loans can be made to government and to commercial borrowers. These can be secured debentures. Income from these instruments is generally fixed and regular, providing guaranteed income, especially from those issuers with the highest credit rating. Debt securities will demonstrate a range of risks depending on the standing of the borrower.

Equity shares

Investments in shares of commercial companies are counted here. This can be another way of offering finance or can represent a bank taking a stake in a commercial venture for its own benefit. Generally, in the UK, this form of financing is left to specialist investors. In Germany, however, it is a normal part of the SME banking market to see ownership of companies on a bank balance sheet. Whilst returns can be high, so are the risks when compared with secured lending.

Interests in joint ventures and associated undertakings

Shareholdings in Visa (credit cards) or other payments organisations are shown here. On numerous occasions banks enter into joint ventures (ATM networks/cheque processing/plastic card schemes) and record the investment in their accounts. These shareholdings are often too small in terms of % ownership to allow full incorporation into group accounts.

Intangible fixed assets – goodwill

In accounting terms this is the amount by which the bank's total assets exceed its physical and financial assets because of its reputation. This figure will usually be calculated with reference to the price paid to take over a brand name.

Tangible fixed assets

Branches, Head Office premises, computer hardware and furniture are represented here. Generally these do not provide an income stream to the bank but are essential in its activities.

Other assets

This includes pre-payments and expenses that a bank has made in advance and interest and charges accrued that customers have not paid yet.

Retail life fund assets attributable to policyholders.

This is self-explanatory and is matched by a corresponding entry under liabilities. The assets are in the form of investments (stocks, shares, property) that belong, legally to life policy holders. The bank cannot use these assets for its own purposes.

The theme to remember when reviewing a bank balance sheet is the riskiness of assets – the chance that the bank could lose some or all of their value. When that happens the bank must be able to summon enough funds from its own capital resources to cover the liabilities that fund the poor quality assets. This is because the depositors (liabilities) may want their money back and the bank has to be able to pay them or lose the trust of the market. Chapter 5 deals in detail with this aspect of regulation and capital adequacy.

In the example given in fig. 3.1 it is difficult to be precise about the risks associated with every asset but in general the following will hold true:

Figure 3.2: The riskiness of banking assets

ASSETS	INDICATIVE RISK	COMMENTS
Cash & balances at central banks	LOW	Physical risks of theft only
Items in course of collection	LOW	These are "owed" by other clearing banks
Treasury & other bills	LOW	Government debt is, in theory, risk free
Loans and advances to banks	LOW?	This will depend on the bank but lending only to high credit rated banks will lower risk
Loans and advances to customers	LOW TO MEDIUM	This depends on credit assessment and the taking of security
Debt securities	LOW TO MEDIUM	Normally secured but asset prices can drop
Equity shares	HIGH	Equity capital is also called risk capital
Joint ventures	MEDIUM	This also depends on the nature of the joint venture.
Fixed assets	LOW	Risks against fire and flood can be insured

You will note that over 70% of assets in our typical bank balance sheet have higher risk than the remaining 30%. These are the assets that also have the greatest profit potential. Government debt (low risk), for example, will carry the lowest interest rate achievable at the time of issue. Treasury bonds, which are used to regulate bank liquidity, are offered at the repo rate, also known as the Minimum Lending Rate. This is explained more fully in Chapter 4.

Liabilities

The profit-earning assets above need to be financed and there are limitations to the extent to which banks can do this from their own reserves. The liabilities side of the balance sheet clearly illustrates that a bank, to be successful and profitable, must also select a mixture of different financing types that, themselves, have different costs and characteristics.

Figure 3.3: Liabilities in a typical bank balance sheet

	£M	% OF TOTAL LIABILITIES
Liabilities		
Deposits by banks	93,201	20.9
Customer accounts	198,116	44.3
Debt securities	48,431	10.8
Items in course of collection	1,662	0.4
Other liabilities	68,869	15.4
Dated & undated loan capital	12,553	2.8
Capital		
Minority interests	193	0.0
Share capital (called up)	1,638	0.4
Reserves	14,426	3.2
Retail life funds	7,642	1.7
TOTAL LIABILITIES	446,731	

The liabilities shown above are:

Deposits by banks

Banks deposit funds with other banks via the inter-bank market in order to maximise the return on funds held (sometimes overnight). This also maintains liquidity in the markets.

Customer accounts

These are funds deposited in current and savings accounts. For larger savings transactions (over £50,000) Certificates of Deposit (CDs) can be issued. These are negotiable and can be traded. These form the largest source of funding and can cost the bank the least. Funds held on current account will attract a very low interest rate (or no interest at all) and will cost the bank only the physical costs of collecting the funds via the branch network.

Debt securities in issue

These are loans to the bank held by or purchased by other financial institutions. As a good credit risk the bank can expect to pay very favourable rates of interest.

Items in the course of collection due to other banks

This is the corresponding entry to the asset side. These are cheques collected by other banks drawn on the particular bank by its customers. Net indebtedness is covered on a daily basis (excluding bank holidays and weekends) by transfer between accounts of banks at the Bank of England.

Other liabilities

This figure covers expenses accrued that have not yet been paid, interest on accounts that has not yet been paid to customers and provisions for bad and doubtful debts. Where a bank fails to receive full repayment of a loan, perhaps due to insolvency, it funds the shortfall from its own profits. This figure includes provisions that the bank may have to fund in the future.

Dated and undated loan capital

These are debentures used by the bank to raise capital. They are largely owned by other financial institutions. Once again interest rates paid will be the lowest acceptable to raise the funding at the time of issue.

Minority interests

This is the proportion of the bank's profit that is due to outside shareholders in subsidiary companies that are not wholly owned by the bank.

Called-up share capital

These are the equity shares in issue. Many of these will be held by private investors and staff (as part of profit-sharing schemes) but the majority will be held by other financial institutions as sound investments for their fund-holders.

Reserves

This represents the major part of a bank's capital and is an accumulation of retained profits over the years. These, and the bank's equity, represent most of the Tier 1 capital under the Basel 1 accord (see Chapter 6).

Retail life fund liabilities attributable to policyholders

This is the corresponding entry to the assets. These monies are owed (and will eventually be paid) to policyholders.

Profitability

The nature of intermediation and the motivation of each party to the process are key to understanding the series of dilemmas facing banks when deciding on the balance of asset and liability types. Banks must provide profits, good returns for customers and a good enough credit rating for the bank to enable it to borrow funds from other banks at the lowest possible rates. Associated with this is the need to reduce physical costs (maintaining a branch network and staffing).

Whilst it will be relatively easy for banks to set interest rates for borrowers higher than their cost of funds plus overhead costs these rates must also be competitive in order to attract liabilities (lenders) and assets (borrowers) in the first place. To ensure a positive margin a bank can offer only fixed rates to depositors and borrowers but then it misses the opportunity to make higher profits if short-term rates change. To ensure that it benefits from short-term interest rate movements a bank can offer only variable rates (a percentage above LIBOR or its own base rate) but then it misses the opportunity to achieve higher profits on larger, longer-term loans and may be uncompetitive in the market for larger longer-term deposits.

Profitability, measured by **Return on Equity (ROE)** will also be affected by bank regulation – not only the physical costs of compliance but the capital requirements based on the type of business that the bank transacts (see Chapter 5).

Figure 3.4 estimates ROE based on assumptions about:
- Capital requirements
- Interest spread
- Fees and commissions
- Cost/income ratio
- Expected loan losses
- Tax rate
- Interest spread and fees will be driven as much by competition in specific markets as by the lending policy adopted by a particular bank. Although banks maintain and fix their own preferred margins, transparency of interest

rates, especially for consumer products, is essential and this can lead to a lack of differentiation between providers.

▷ Fees and commissions arise from loans and also from non-interest products such as insurance, handling fees for foreign exchange etc. In order to protect fixed interest rate offers there can be "booking" fees as well as early repayment penalties.

▷ Cost/income ratios rely largely on staffing and premises. Traditional branch networks are far more expensive than internet only banks but can miss opportunities for economies of scope – building a relationship based on the brand strength and market presence.

▷ Chapters 11 and 12 of this text review common issues in credit appraisal and debt recovery. However careful and prudent the initial lending decision the element of risk apparent makes it certain that some loans will never be repaid. Even with house mortgages, the value of the security can fall so that the whole of the loan is not covered (a phenomenon called "negative equity").

Figure 3.4: Estimating ROE

The figures in this table are based on a single £100,000 house mortgage loan with a capital requirement of 4% (£4,000). Watch the annual ROE figure as the different assumptions listed above are changed.

ASSUMPTIONS	SCENARIO A	SCENARIO B	SCENARIO C	SCENARIO D
Capital requirement	4%	4%	4%	4%
Interest spread	3%	2%	2%	2%
Loan fee	2%	1%	1%	1%
Cost Income ratio	50%	50%	50%	60%
Loan losses	1%	1%	2%	2%
Taxation rate	26%	26%	26%	26%
ROE	**28%**	**9%**	**-9%**	**-15%**

Scenario A is the base case where the bank has benign economic conditions and little competition. Scenario B introduces competition through the narrowing of the interest spread achieved and reduction of loan fees. Scenario C introduces economic problems and increased loan losses and Scenario D reflects increased costs of delivery.

The model could go on to assume different capital and tax requirements but the key point is made – that bank profits can be fragile and affected by a wide range of issues that banks must balance and manage on a daily basis.

Chapter 8 deals with "economies of scope" – or the opportunity for banks to build on the basic creditor/debtor relationship and to sell banking products. Commissions and fees (less compensation for mis-selling – see Chapter 2) are responsible for about half of retail bank profits annually.

Physical costs of operations and staff are also vital to bank profitability. In Chapter 9 some of the delivery system choices are described as banks seek to reduce costs and increase efficiencies.

Liquidity

Some general rules indicate the complexity of the balance that the bank must perform:

1. Depositors want good returns but want to be able to withdraw their funds on demand.
2. Borrowers want to enjoy low rates of interest and long repayment periods.
3. The longer the repayment period the riskier the loan (more chance for risks to change) and the higher the interest rate required. Some loans are defaulted and never repaid in full (see Chapter 11 for more about credit risk).
4. The longer the period of deposit the higher the interest rate required (depositors want compensation for tying up their funds for longer periods).
5. The more liquid the funds (more easily converted to cash to meet withdrawals) the lower the interest rate and the profit margin.
6. The less liquid the funds the higher interest rate can be charged or received.
7. Interest rates change over time based on inflation, monetary policy decisions, market conditions and expectations.

The delicate balance achieved by banks on a daily basis is beyond the scope of this text but it is enough to realise the complexity of this area. Get it wrong on interest rates and the bank may post a loss, especially where overhead costs are high. Also the bank may run out of cash if it lends long-term but borrows only short-term to finance this. This is not only a problem for the bank but for the whole financial system as the intermediary nature of banking creates such inter-dependence. The main strategy for managing liquidity risk will be maintaining a wide portfolio of assets and liabilities with different maturities and different liquidity characteristics (ease of conversion to cash).

And – we have not even considered movements in exchange rates that will impact banks where loans and deposits are made in different currencies.

These issues look and are highly complex but may be made clearer by reference to a basic example. In this example Countryside Bank plc has agreed a £1 million secured loan for one year at a fixed interest rate of 4%. The loan will be repaid after 12 months on the sale of the property it is used to purchase.

The bank has a choice of methods by which to finance the loan as summarised in Figure 3.5:

Figure 3.5: An example of interest and liquidity risk

LIABILITY (£1M)	RATE (% P.A.)	TERM	COMMENT
Customer deposits	1% variable	On demand	Big profit potential but big liquidity risk as depositors could withdraw their funds tomorrow. The aggregation effect of a large intermediary will reduce this risk.
Term deposit	3.5% fixed	12 months	Potential small profit, provided that the bank's overhead costs and risk premium do not exceed this level. No liquidity risk.
Short term deposit	0.5% (LIBOR)	3 months	Potential profit for the first three months but then the deposit/loan will have to be re-negotiated. For a bank with a good credit-rating this should not be a problem. There is always a risk of interest rates rising in three months' time, however.

When the loan is drawn matched funding of £1 million on the inter-bank market for three months at LIBOR (currently 0.5%) would seem to be a good idea as it can make a reasonable profit. This depends, however, on the expectations for interest rates. If rates are likely to rise then the certainty of the 12-month term deposit might be better. If rates are likely to fall the LIBOR based three month deal allows the flexibility of achieving a lower rate for the subsequent period of the loan and helps to minimise problems if the loan is repaid early.

There is also the possibility of lending the funds at a variable rate (say 2% over LIBOR) but this may limit the market into which such loans can be offered as borrowers seek certainty of outcome too.

Finally, banks can bundle a number of such loans together and "sell" them to another investor for cash ("securitisation"), thus passing the risk and the profit for the loans on to another party in exchange for immediate liquidity. Or banks can engage in interest rate derivatives (futures or swaps) to further limit the potential downside. These last two areas are far too advanced for an introductory text so we'll leave them there.

A credit-crunch case study

In August 2008 the former Building Society, Alliance and Leicester plc, was subject to a buyout by Banco Santander SA, the giant Spanish bank. Credit write-downs and higher funding costs were said to be responsible for a net loss for the first half of 2008 of £23.9m ($47m). Consumer and Commercial profits of £300m ($600m) were wiped out by losses from the Treasury unit.

Like other former building societies, A&L had expanded from its traditional retail/house mortgage base when it became a bank. Also like others (Dunfermline, Bradford and Bingley) its funding strategy added risk rather than reducing it.

"Casino banking", that was partially responsible for the credit-crunch of 2007/08, is set to be separated from the retail banking source of loan assets. More about this in Chapter 5.

Summary

This chapter has covered:
▶ The structure of a bank balance sheet
▶ The nature of and risks associated with assets on a balance sheet
▶ The nature of liabilities on a balance sheet
▶ The impact on profits of key market, regulatory and bank cost factors
▶ The interest rate and liquidity risk parameters that influence asset and liability management by banks.

Further reading and useful web links

Bloomberg – Alliance and Leicester 1 August 2008 – http://www.bloomberg.com/apps/news?pid=newsarchive&sid=adrCRaMzVKBw&refer=uk

British Bankers Association – BBA LIBOR - http://www.bbalibor.com/

Molyneux P and Goacher D, (2005) *The Monetary and Financial System* 6th edn., Global Professional Publishing.

Stoakes C, (2013), *Know the City*-2013/14, Christopher Stoakes Ltd.

Treasury Committee, (2008), *The Run on the Rock*, Vol 1, The Stationery Office.

CHAPTER 4

Retail Banks and the Economy

Objectives

After studying this chapter you should be able to:
- State the four functions of money
- Describe the components of money supply
- Explain the significance of monetary policy for banks
- Describe the monetary activities of Central Banks
- Explain particular areas of banking markets that impact on monetary policy

Introduction

The importance and central nature of banking in modern economies is outlined in this chapter. The pursuit of monetary policy via central banks (Bank of England BoE/European Central Bank ECB/Federal Reserve FED/Monetary Authority of Singapore MAS etc.) is described and the position of banks in this process reviewed. Recent trends in such areas as house mortgage finance and consumer credit are also reviewed.

This chapter builds on earlier discussions about the nature of the banking system and the creation of credit, a major input to the supply of money. This is not meant to be an economics text but hopes to place the banks in context within the monetary system since without them, government policy would not run smoothly. The chapter also paves the way for the next chapter in this section of the text as it underlines the importance to the authorities of stability in the financial system – a feature that bank regulation strives to achieve.

Money

In this chapter it is important to determine what money is so that we can have a working definition of what actually flows through the financial system. Demand for and supply of money grows and contracts and impacts the growth of the economy, inflation and exchange rates.

Money is anything that fulfils FOUR main functions:

▶ A medium of exchange (acceptable to all, divisible, convenient, secure etc.)
▶ A liquid store of value
▶ A unit of account, and
▶ A standard of deferred payments

Stories abound whereby cowrie shells, bird of paradise feathers and other recognisable but rare objects were used as currencies by isolated peoples. The fact is that as long as a society agrees that a certain object is treated as money (and it holds the above FOUR attributes) then it is money. As soon as the society and its government lose control of the money supply it becomes useless.

A medium of exchange

Instead of swapping goods for goods (barter) we exchange goods for money and then the money for other goods. Money acts as an intermediary (a **medium of exchange**) just as banks act as intermediaries between borrowers and lenders. The bank is an acceptable counterparty to both whilst the borrower individually may not be acceptable to the individual lender. Without all the exchanges of goods and services made possible by money, we would have to be much more self-sufficient and hence endure a lower standard of living as the benefits of exchange would not accrue.

Normally a nation's own currency is the most acceptable and there is good business to be done by banks in providing customers and tourists with the possibility of exchanging their "home" currency with the national currency (and back again) when foreign travel is undertaken.

Case study – Ukraine from 1992

It is interesting to note that when inflation, war or economic collapse affect a nation the local currency can become devalued and distrusted. Citizens can seek certainty in so-called "reserve" currencies such as the US dollar or the euro. One example is that of Ukraine, formerly part of the Soviet Union.

In 1992 Ukraine became an independent state once again and re-introduced its pre-1918 currency karbovanets (coupons) in place of Soviet roubles. However, the economy was weak and inflation grew, making the value and buying power of karbovanets decrease rapidly. Citizens turned to the familiar US dollar as a trusted medium of exchange. Despite the holding and use of US dollars being illegal in Ukraine the practice was widespread. By 1996 economic reforms and stability had been introduced and the nation introduced its present currency, the gryvnia (pronounced "grivna"). The new and old currencies were exchanged at a fixed rate, helping the new currency to become accepted. The authorities began to actively control the use of US dollar until the Hryvnia was fully accepted.

This continued until the global financial crisis made it impossible for the National Bank of Ukraine to continue to maintain a pegged exchange rate with the US dollar and the Hryvnia devalued once again.

A liquid store of value

Money is also a reasonable **liquid store of value**, by which we mean we can save it fairly easily. The word 'liquid' is used because most bank and building society deposits can be very easily changed into notes and coins without delay, without any cost and with no loss of capital value or forfeit of interest . After all, that's the definition of liquidity – a characteristic of an asset which is able to be converted into cash quickly at minimum cost and with minimum loss. Try selling an antique sofa and see how much hassle there is with such an illiquid asset! Houses and company stocks and shares can often be good stores of value, for old age or sickness, but they are highly illiquid as they are costly to dispose of and you have to wait for your money. A general "liquidity spectrum" is illustrated in Figure 4.1:

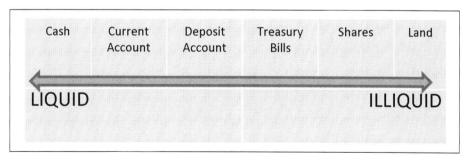

Figure 4.1   The liquidity spectrum

A unit of account

Thirdly, money is a **unit of account.** We use money to add together all sorts of completely different items, for reasons of clarity and brevity, to help us calculate:
- Total values of all the assorted articles;
- Figures for the profit or loss we have made on the transactions in the past year;
- Budget totals of expenditure beyond which we may not go in the coming year;
- Forecasts of sales/profits which we expect to achieve during the coming year.

In other words, and not surprisingly, we are using money for accounting, management information and targeting.

A standard of deferred payment

Lastly, money has the quality of a **standard of deferred payment**. We defer payment by offering to pay money, usually over a much longer period. A house mortgage loan is a good example of this. Here we are using money for banking and legal purposes, incorporating money values in the contract, agreeing to pay at some date in the future. Of course, interest reflects the value to the borrower of the deferment in terms of liquidity given up (the lender cannot spend it twice!) and the risk that repayment will not be complete..

The importance of defining money and knowing what is acceptable as money is that we need money to trade. Trade or economic exchange drives economic growth and it is this that makes us and individual countries wealthier (provided inflation is restrained). Governments around the world have similar policy aims – to ensure steady stable growth in the economy. A focus on the supply of money is central to the work of the monetary authorities as part of that growth objective.

The supply of money

The **money supply** can be measured in a number of different ways and their definitions are decided by central governments and central banks. Its growth and predicted movement are closely observed by banks in order to promote stability as data makes predictions and forward planning more accurate.

In 2013 the newly appointed Governor of the Bank of England, Mark Carney, repeated a strategy he had used successfully in Canada – Forward Guidance. Rather than increase it, a period of low interest rates can limit investment. Borrowers and investors share a fear that rates will rise, making marginal projects unprofitable. By benchmarking a rise in rates to unemployment levels the Governor explicitly indicated that rates would remain low for the short to medium term (barring external shocks).

The important measures of money supply are M0 and M4. Every so often changes are made with some measures being altered, others abolished and sometimes one or two are renumbered. In the UK major changes took place in 1987, after the Building Societies Act 1986, and again in 1989 after the Abbey National became a bank. The latter change caused the disappearance of the M1, M3 and M3c measures, which may feature in books written before 1989.

All major economies use and publish money supply totals although regulatory and industry differences between nations mean that the definitions of the various money aggregates are not directly comparable. Figure 4.2 offers a broad definition of the key monetary measures:

Figure 4.2: Definitions of monetary aggregates

MONETARY AGGREGATE	DEFINITION	COMMENTS
M0	Notes and coins with the general public	Also called "narrow money"
MB	M0 plus notes and coins in the tills and cash dispensers of the banks and building societies and the operational balances of banks at the Central Bank	"Monetary Base"
M1	M0 plus demand deposits and the balances of checking accounts.	
M2	M1 plus savings and time deposits of individuals.	
M3/4	Institutional deposits and larger liquid assets and Money Market funds.	"Broad Money" or "Money Supply"

M0 is important as it measures rises and falls in holdings of cash as interest rates change. In this way economists can gauge the likely effect of a rate change on at least this part of the money supply. In the UK, however, the definition includes bank vault cash and reserve deposits – although others, such as the USA refer to this as the Base Money (MB).

M4, by contrast, is the major measure in the UK of "broad" money. It comprises:
▷ Notes and coin with the general public (the first part of MB).

▶ All deposits in sterling from residents with banks and building societies.

▶ In India M4 also includes savings in Post Office Savings accounts, reflecting the importance of this mechanism in that particular economy.

All of the above measures exclude money held by the government and by overseas residents, so, when we pay taxes to the government by deduction from our salary or by cheque, the money supply falls. When the government pays the wages of civil servants, the money supply rises. When sterling is used to pay overseas traders for the goods we import from them, the money supply also falls.

From the above it is important to see that money is not a "stock" that can be measured but a "flow" – one person's deposit becomes a loan in the hands of a banking intermediary. The monetary authorities are not only interested in the measure of M0 or M4 but also the speed with which it flows around the economy. The faster the "flow" and the greater the number of transactions, the higher the level of money in the money supply. Innovations such as Smart cards, NETS, EPOS etc. all impact on the speed of the "flow".

Inflation

Inflation was described in the 1980s as "Public Enemy Number One" and many attempts have been made over the years to reduce its negative effects in order to promote stable economic growth. Inflation can spiral out of control and instances of this in the past have led to a huge devaluation in the value of money, distrust of cash in favour of "real" assets and the collapse of economic activity.

In the 1920s in Germany's Weimar Republic and again in the 1990s in Serbia the local currency suffered through hyperinflation, was massively devalued and distrusted by the population. Preference was for barter, direct exchange of goods and use of scarce but trusted foreign currencies. Nothing like this has ever happened in the UK but even low levels of inflation can have serious effects:

▶ Confidence in money as a measure of value erodes.

▶ The value of savings erodes and may fall in real terms where the interest paid is less than the rate of inflation (in this instance many people would rather hold their money in cash).

▶ The rich get richer and the poor poorer. Wage earners can bargain for more wages if prices rise whilst those on fixed incomes (benefits or pensions) get relatively worse off.

▶ Investor confidence erodes and so future economic growth stalls. Investors will invest in other countries where inflation is lower.

▶ Exports look relatively more expensive and the economy suffers as foreign exchange earnings reduce.

Inflation is inextricably linked with any discussion about money as it relates to the phenomenon of "too much money chasing too few goods", or the supply of money and the ability of individuals to make purchases outstrips the availability of real goods to purchase. House price inflation is but one aspect of this as the availability of mortgage loans far exceeds the housing stock on the market. This inevitably leads to the prices of those houses rising in money terms. In real terms the houses are worth the same.

Restrictions on mortgage lending can also, of course, have a reverse effect and house prices can fall in the short term as banks and other lenders improve the quality of their lending by reducing *Loan to Value ratios (LTV)* and demanding deposits from first-time buyers.

Although there are many separate causes of inflation (imported costs rise, wage rises or simply growth in the economy) UK economic policy since 1997 has been firmly focused on the maintenance of inflation within a narrow band of values (currently 1% - 3% p.a. as measured by the *Consumer Price Index*[11] *(CPI)*, i.e. + or - 1% around a central target of 2%).

The central bank

In the UK the Bank of England is the central bank. It has responsibilities relating to economic stability, banking regulation and, importantly the control of inflation via the *Monetary Policy Committee (MPC)*.

The MPC was set up under the Bank of England Act 1998. In this Act it was given responsibility to set interest rates with the overall aim of achieving an inflation target set by the government. The current target is + or - 1% around a central target of 2% CPI. This is a "symmetrical" target as the authorities consider a rate of inflation below 1% to be as damaging as a rate above 3%, since this would denote a slowing of economic growth.

The nine members of the MPC meet monthly and alert the market to their thoughts by publishing minutes of their meetings, including details of individual votes of members. This helps to maintain stability by allowing the markets to form good expectations of future rate changes. Consistency and stability are required if inflation is to be beaten.

As noted earlier, in 2013 the MPC began to issue "forward guidance" as part of its strategy to maintain stability. So far the guidance has been focused on another key measure of economic performance – unemployment. In the future this focus could change.

---

11 The CPI replaced the Retail Prices Index (RPI) as the UK measure of inflation in 2003. It charts a "basket" of ordinary goods but excludes owner occupier housing costs such as mortgage interest payments and buildings insurance. In this way it is more comparable with the index used in the EU, where house ownership is not a prevalent.

Both the symmetrical target and the transparency of the MPC meetings are in stark contrast to the activities of the European Central Bank (ECB) that sets interest rates for the Eurozone. The ECB keeps its meetings secret and economists are less able to forecast rate movements. In addition the ECB tries to keep inflation below 2%, thus allowing deflation to occur if conditions are right.

This background on the MPC is simply to put into context the key tool used to change interest rates – the **repo rate**.

The repo rate is the official rate of interest at which the Bank of England will deal with the short-term money markets. To maintain liquidity in the money markets the Bank buys and sells repos (sale and repurchase agreements) to banks and discount houses who need either to invest surplus funds or borrow in the short-term to balance their books for the day. Although the banks could borrow from other institutions the repo rate is one of the lowest available and represents a guarantee of payment as it is backed by the Bank itself. This is also known as the Bank's "lender of last resort" function.

By funding liquidity shortages in the money markets the Bank can heavily influence the banks' cost of funds and thus their "base rate". The setting of short-term bank interest rates, however, is only part of the influence felt. The MPC itself considers that four key economic factors are influenced by their decisions:

▶ Short and long term bank rates
▶ Asset prices
▶ Expectations, and
▶ Exchange rates

The impact on **short term interest rates** is clear. If the cost of funds to a bank goes up then it will pass on this increase in costs to its customers by way of higher interest rates. Note here that because building societies derive a far lower proportion of their funding from the wholesale markets they are less influenced by MPC rate changes.

A big proportion of bank borrowing for house mortgage is at variable rates and so these too will be influenced. With more to pay on mortgages individuals will have less to spend and so a rate rise might "cool" the economy and help to dampen inflation when it works through. A similar effect is expected on credit card borrowing although it is thought that a large increase in interest rates is needed to make a significant difference in demand for credit here.

The impact on long-term rates is more difficult to forecast as this will depend also on expectations of future rate rises or cuts.

Asset prices will usually fall as interest rates rise (and vice versa). So, again, a rate rise by the MPC will help to prevent **asset price inflation**. An example of this is houses. If it is more expensive to borrow for house purchase fewer people will demand houses and prices will not rise as fast (they may even fall in the short term). Also share prices may fall as higher interest rates paid on savings makes these investments appear more attractive than holding shares.

The way in which the MPC believes their policy is transmitted to the inflation rate is summarised in Figure 4.3:

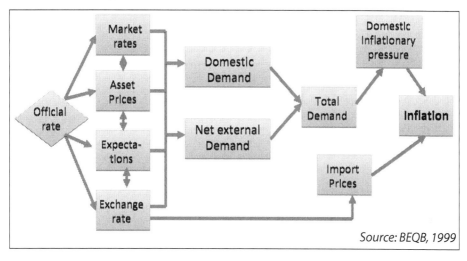

Source: BEQB, 1999

Figure 4.3: The transmission mechanism of monetary policy

Peoples' expectations about interest and inflation will be influenced by their understanding of the MPC's actions, supported by the publication of minutes. Does a rate rise mean another to follow or is a small rise enough?

Finally exchange rates will be heavily influenced by **interest rates** as it is interest rates that determine forward rates that support trade. In addition, higher interest rates will attract foreign investment in the UK as higher returns are available. As euro, dollar or yen balances are exchanged for sterling to invest in the UK more sterling is demanded and its price rises (**exchange rate**). This makes imports relatively cheaper and so helps to keep inflation down in this way. Unfortunately it also makes exports to other countries more expensive and so builds up pressures elsewhere in the economy, especially amongst exporting companies who may shed jobs or lose income.

Taken together it is estimated that the MPC decisions take about 12 months to influence demand for goods and services and a full two years to impact on inflation. The MPC is always, therefore, looking two years ahead and does not expect instant responses to its decisions as far as inflation is concerned.

Quantitative easing

Up until 2007, in the UK, US and Eurozone, interest rates were the central bankers' key tool in managing the inflation target (and money supply target in the case of the ECB). However, with the onset of low interest rates in the wake of the banking crisis the effectiveness of changes in interest rates was much reduced and central banks sought other mechanisms.

The key mechanism used was **Quantitative Easing (QE)**. This was first used by the Bank of Japan in an attempt to combat deflation in the early 2000s, when interest rates were set at zero.

QE has the same aim as interest rate manipulation in that it attempts to affect the liquidity in the banking system by purchasing assets from financial institutions for cash ("printing money" as some critics call it). It works to increase the credit available to individuals and businesses provided that the banks are willing to lend. Thus, QE can be accompanied by government loan guarantee schemes, mortgage subsidy and SME initiatives in order to stimulate growth.

QE works through the same channels as interest rate changes (see Figure 4.3) impacting on asset prices and exchange rates as well as expectations but doing so via the banks' ability and willingness to lend rather than through the pricing of loans (interest).

It is too early to tell whether QE since 2007 has had a positive effect on growth but the policy makers were probably wise to adopt it as, in its absence, the recession may have been even more protracted.

Key issues in credit creation – a UK example

Although the above is a very brief and swift tour of some very important economic areas the intention of this text is to put banks in the context of policy decisions rather than provide a full economic discussion far better left to economics texts.

Three key retail banking issues that are both influenced by and, in turn, influence UK monetary policy are:
- The UK housing and mortgage market
- UK credit card debt
- Business borrowing

Two key features of the UK housing market are of note and these are the preponderance of owner-occupiers (much higher than in Europe) and the fact that most house mortgage loans are agreed at variable rates.

The demand for house ownership exerts influence on the demand for mortgage funding and in earlier chapters we saw that retail banks now dominate this market with building societies in second place as providers. Since the borrowing is secured on domestic property the capital requirement under Basel accords (see next chapter) is lower than for ordinary borrowing.

This does mean, however, that much household borrowing is linked to the repo rate and can, therefore, fluctuate as rates change. This can mean that for borrowers who stretch their finances to borrow enough to afford a house, a rise in interest rates of even 0.25% can be unaffordable. This will have repercussions for other commitments such as credit card debt repayment.

The credit-crunch and banking crisis saw mortgage rates fall and then stall as the cost of funds to banks became cheaper but their need to cover overhead costs and achieve a margin for profit created a minimum mortgage rate offered.

One other feature of home ownership is that individuals have more confidence about the economy if house prices are rising as they feel wealthier. This can encourage longer-term decisions such as borrowing on credit cards or personal loans, even if their income is only just sufficient to meet repayments.

UK credit card debt is said to be the highest in Europe. It is unsecured and exceeds £1 trillion. Pressures from the housing market and from interest rate changes can influence the level of borrowing and, in time, bad debts. The ease with which people can enter bankruptcy and wipe out their debts (legally) is often cited as a bad omen for credit cards but the fact is that most borrowers are honest and trustworthy, though possibly foolish, and fully intend to repay their debts.

The incidence of borrowing is no less significant in the business area as well. With low and stable rates of interest and economic growth and inflation businesses are motivated to invest or grow or extend their services in some way. Much of the time this is done with bank borrowing, leasing or asset finance. Whatever name it is called it is borrowing that must be repaid at some time and attracts interest. High borrowing on a business balance sheet is often the cause of business failure as economic conditions or market forces can limit the ability of a firm to repay debt.

So far government initiatives to encourage banks to lend to small- and medium-sized businesses, in particular, have not had the success anticipated. The credit environment appears to be too fragile for banks to lend or for businesses to require finance.

We live in a credit-driven society, where high house prices, low inflation and social norms all make us feel easier about borrowing.

In the 2007 edition of this book the following sentence completed this chapter:

> *Just how sensible economic growth based on credit is*
> *will become apparent if an external shock (say oil prices*
> *doubling as they did in the 1970s) happens.*

The sub-prime crisis in the US provided just such an external shock as it was generated outside the UK but swiftly permeated our financial system through the complex and interdependent links created by the inter-bank financing of these bad loans. The years since then have shown that consumer and business confidence can be shaken, house prices and other asset prices can re-balance but that the continuing mantra of economic growth will allow such memories to fade.

Summary

This chapter has covered:
- ▶ Money and its key functions
- ▶ The money supply
- ▶ Inflation and its effects
- ▶ Monetary policy in the UK
- ▶ The position of banks in the economy

Further reading and useful web links

Bank of England, (1999), The transmission mechanism of monetary policy, *Bank of England Quarterly Bulletin*, May pp 161 – 170

Bank of England website at: http://www.bankofengland.co.uk/monetarypolicy/Pages/default.aspx

And at http://www.bankofengland.co.uk/monetarypolicy/Pages/qe/default.aspx

CHAPTER 5

Retail Banking Regulation

Objectives

After studying this chapter you should be able to:

▷ Explain why regulation of financial services is needed in an economy

▷ Explain the different types of regulation apparent in retail banking

▷ Describe the key features of the THREE Basel accords

▷ Describe the various types of risk that bankers face

▷ Discuss the ways in which risk can be measured and mitigated

▷ Discuss the implications of the credit-crunch for financial services regulation.

Introduction

Banks are amongst the most closely monitored and regulated commercial companies in any economy. Their central role in monetary policy transmission and in the growth of an economy argues strongly for them to be stable and not to risk loss by making reckless decisions. Such regulation and supervision, however, must be tempered with the knowledge that these are commercial companies with duties to their shareholders to be profitable.

In this chapter global regulation under the Basel accords is outlined and examples of national regulation by central banks and key regulators are offered to illustrate key points. The overall focus is on risks. Different types of banking risk are identified and described.

The chapter ends with some discussion on the implications of the 2007-2009 credit-crunch for regulators and banks.

The need for regulation

There are no certainties in life or in economics and the arguments for regulation of financial services are based largely on economic principles. The fact is that most banks and financial systems in the world are supervised and regulated by national and international authorities to avoid the pitfalls that economic theory suggests lies ahead for the unwary.

Before outlining these cogent arguments, however, it is worth noting that the type of regulation that exists in any one national setting is only one option for the regulators and each nation will advance its own ideas and systems. Different systems, however, will need to be fairly similar ("the level playing field") since large banks may simply open operations in those countries with less demanding regulation (regulatory arbitrage), thus gaining an advantage over banks in more stringent regulatory areas.

It is also worth noting that another school of thought, labelled "free banking" supports the notion that the market itself (forces of supply and demand, competition and survival) will regulate banks adequately. There have been instances of "free banking" in some countries (notably New Zealand) but they have been short-lived experiments as the outside (more regulated) world exerts a strong influence. The credit-crunch provides clear evidence, too, that the market cannot adequately regulate itself and the self preservation motive of banks cannot always be assumed.

So, why do the governmental and monetary authorities want to regulate financial institutions so closely?

The answer lies in our understanding of the economy and the money flows within it, including the creation of credit and the essential trust that we show in banks, particularly, before we invest our life savings in them. All of these points have been covered elsewhere in this text. What regulation strives to avoid are the problems associated with:

- Bank failure (where the failure of one bank through recklessness or bad management or bad luck has repercussions for the whole banking system and the whole economy).
- Asymmetry of information (where customers and banks have private information that changes the risk profile of the other party – to their disadvantage).
- A lack of competition and fairness in financial markets (where the activities of those banks dominating a market can limit choice).

Regulation can be divided into THREE main types of intervention by regulators:

1. Systematic Regulation
2. Prudential Regulation
3. Conduct of Business Regulation

Systematic regulation

Systematic regulation refers to those measures adopted at national (e.g. UK with the privatisation of RBS and Lloyds Banking Group) or currency area level (e.g. European Union in relation to Greece, Spain, Italy and Portugal) and aimed at limiting bank failures, contagion within the system as well as consumer protection.

Central banks acting as "lender of last resort" – see Chapter 4 – support liquidity in banking markets on a daily basis. More specific to retail banks, however, is deposit insurance – or deposit protection schemes that offer a state guarantee (up to a certain limit) of compensation should an individual bank fail and be unable to meet its obligations to repay depositors. Figure 5.1 summarises the different limits applied around the world:

Figure 5.1: Deposit insurance scheme limits – selected countries

COUNTRY / CURRENCY AREA	MAXIMUM COMPENSATION*	£ EQUIVALENT AS AT AUGUST 2013
Australia	A$250,000	£144,115
Ireland	unlimited	unlimited
Europe and Eurozone (most countries)	€100,000	£85,362
Hong Kong	HK$500,000	£41,546
Russia	RUB700,000	£13,571
Singapore	S$50,000	£25,279
Switzerland	CHF100,000	£69,245
UK	£85,000	£85,000
USA	$250,000	£161,108

* *Normally compensation is on a per individual and per institution basis and so an individual can get more protection by splitting deposits between banks. Foreign currency deposits are not normally covered.*

During the credit crunch of 2007-2009 many regulators and governments raised maxima and even removed them completely for limited periods in order to calm fears of bank runs. In the above figure Ireland is alone in maintaining an unlimited level of protection into 2013.

Prudential regulation – The Basel Accords

Since 1988 banks and national regulators have worked within the *accord* set out by the Basel Committee of Central Banks, meeting in Basel, Switzerland. The Committee wanted to ensure that all banks maintained enough capital to cover the various risks and losses they were undertaking anywhere in the world. The system also allowed for a "level playing field" so that smaller banks could compete with larger ones on a more equal footing.

The accord – outlined below – was replaced in 2007 by Basel 2 and subsequently by Basel 3, a far more sophisticated system of supervision to reflect the increased sophistication of banks. Although the new accord is in place, however, the more basic (some say crude) system provides a clearer insight into the concept of capital adequacy. Indeed the basic version of Basel 2 is not dissimilar to the Basel 1 regime.

Basel 1

The key to the system is to maintain **capital adequacy**. This means that each bank must have sufficient capital to match at least 8% of its risk-weighted assets. Reference should now be made to Chapter 3 where the key assets in a bank balance sheet were discussed.

Capital

Capital is the balancing figure in a balance sheet and relates to the difference between assets and liabilities. It also represents the "shareholders' funds". For the purposes of the accord it is split into Tier 1 and Tier 2 capital:

- ▷ Tier 1 includes shareholders' equity and disclosed reserves.
- ▷ Tier 2 includes undisclosed reserves, subordinated debt and general provisions (profits put aside to cover potential bad loans).
- ▷ At least 50% of capital must be Tier 1.

Risk weighted assets

Risk weighted assets are the earning assets of the bank – remember from Chapter 3, the higher the risk the higher the return.

Under Basel 1, assets are weighted as follows:

CASH	0%
Gilts or OECD government debt	20%
Mortgages to owner occupiers	50%
Commercial loans	100%

These are, indeed, crude measures. The 100% weighting for commercial loans takes no account of the individual creditworthiness of borrowers (who may be other banks with AAA credit ratings) or whether any security has been taken. This is partly why Basel 2 was needed.

The following illustration (Figure 5.2) of the fictitious Countryside Bank plc shows a typical retail bank with a mix of personal and commercial business. In common with other commercial banks Countryside will want to use its capital as efficiently as possible in order to provide the best return for its shareholders within the capital adequacy limits.

Figure 5.2: Capital adequacy under Basel 1

Countryside Bank plc has the following assets (risk-weighted):

ASSET TYPE	£M	RISK WEIGHT (%)	£M
Cash	1,500	0	0
Government and OECD debt	7,500	20	1,500
Domestic mortgages	50,000	50	25,000
Loans to other banks	15,000	100	15,000
Corporate loans	100,000	100	100,000
Personal loans	20,000	100	20,000
TOTALS	**194,000**		**161,500**

Thus, Countryside Bank plc needs at least £161,500m x 8% = **£12,920m** of Capital to fit the Basel criteria. At least **£6,460** (50%) of the Capital must be Equity and Reserves.

Countryside Bank plc has capital of:

TYPE	£M	%
Shareholders" equity	1,500	
Reserves (retained profit)	8,500	
Tier 1 total	**10,000**	**6.2%**
Subordinated debt	5,000	
General provisions	1,500	
Tier 2 total	6,500	
TOTAL	**16,500**	**10.2%**

Thus, it more than covers the Basel requirements.

NB: Most UK banks maintain a Tier 1 ratio of 8% and a RAR of 10 – 15%.

By maintaining profits and boosting reserves banks can supply enough capital to increase their lending activities whilst still maintaining the Basel 1 ratios. Setting aside profits in good times to meet potential bad debts can also boost capital in Tier 2. Thus Basel is designed to encourage banks to act prudently and not to overextend their lending activity.

The credit crunch came when banks were transitioning from Basel 1 to Basel 2 and so many had insufficient capital to absorb losses.

However, the fact that Basel 1 does not differentiate between good credit risks and poorer ones, allocating them all a 100% risk weighting, means that there is potential for some banks to take higher risks than others and actually be less prudent. Risks in a banks liquidity position are not covered at all under the Accord.

Key implications of early regulation (as well as market pressures) encouraged banks to widen their portfolios of activity and to grow their balance sheets so that risks could be spread and even reduced (larger banks should get better credit ratings and finer rates on loans to them). The imposition of Basel 1, spelling out minimum capital requirements, also encouraged banks to grow and a favoured method for this was merger. Thus, regulation based on capital strength will lead to increased concentration in the industry.

Nor did Basel 1 cover "off balance sheet" risks, for example, securitised debt bundled up and packaged in **Special Purpose Vehicles (SPVs)** for onward sale to investors.

At a market level the types of business conducted could also be skewed by regulation. For example, Basel 1 is partly to blame for the increased interest of UK banks in the house mortgage market. For half of the capital required to back lending to commercial borrowers the bank could lend to house mortgage borrower since these assets are weighted at 50% and 100% respectively for risk. Combined with building society deregulation the motivation and the opportunity for banks to buy building societies was ever present.

Since Basel 1 does not differentiate between secured debt to companies and unsecured debt, banks could also extend more unsecured debt (at a higher risk but higher return) for the same level of capital requirement. Overall risks in banking and in the economy could grow and the sensitivity to interest changes magnified.

Basel 2

To meet the more complex financing needs of banks and to further safeguard the financial system a new Basel Accord was agreed. It was far more complex than its predecessor and provides a number of options as regards the level of regulation depending on the size and complexity of the bank involved. For example, HSBC is a "universal bank" operating globally and would have the most sophisticated level of regulation. A small "Savings and Loan" bank in the US mid-west, that only operates locally, would have a very basic level of supervision.

Basel 2 also recognises that the best risk management happens within banks themselves and so, if a bank can show that its own risk management is appropriate the regulator will not impose further restrictions.

Basel 2 has advantages and disadvantages for banks. One clear concern in the years before it came into force was the cost of compliance and the additional systems that banks needed to set up purely to measure the factors that the accord concerned itself with. A potential disadvantage (highlighted by the credit crunch) was seen to be pro-cyclicality. In a recession banks, instead of lending more to aid recovery, would be constrained to lend less as credit risks and credit ratings around the world deteriorated.

Banks could also see benefits, however. The larger banks could see that their capital could be used more efficiently since arbitrary risk measures would be replaced by bespoke ones, often generated by their own in-house systems.

The credit crunch of 2007 – 2009 showed limitations in Basel 2, however. There was still no emphasis on liquidity adequacy.

Three Pillars

Basel 2 is built on three "pillars" as illustrated in Figure 5.3:

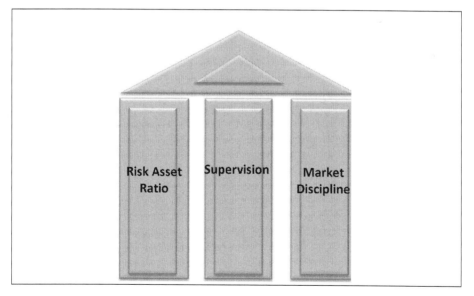

Figure 5.3: The three pillars of Basel 2

1. Risk disclosure of information (also known as market discipline)

Together these three pillars will ensure that all foreseen risks in banks are covered by appropriate discipline, systems and procedures and capital.

Three Options

Basel 2 also gives banks three options for implementation, depending on their size, international reach and the complexity of their business.

1. The standardised approach (a slightly more sophisticated version of Basel 1)
2. Internal Ratings Based approach (where banks use their own risk management systems and allow supervisors to vet them and receive reports on them), And
3. The Advanced Internal Ratings Based approach (more sophisticated than 2).

Capital adequacy is still the key element of the accord but it is the way in which the various banking assets are risk assessed and weighted that can benefit larger banks and restrict smaller ones. Using the example in Figure 5.2 the following illustration (Figure 5.4) attempts to compare the impact of the two accords:

Figure 5.4: Capital Adequacy under Basel 2.

ASSET TYPE	£M	%	£M	COMMENT
Cash	1,500	0	0	
Government and OECD debt	7,500	20	1,500	
Domestic mortgages (secured)	50,000	25	12,500	Risk is calculated with reference to historic default
Loans to other banks	15,000	20	3,000	Only highly credit rated banks receive loans.
Corporate loans (secured)	100,000	30	30,000	Risk is calculated as above
Personal loans	20,000	50	10,000	Normally unsecured
TOTALS	**194,000**		**57,000**	

Thus, Countryside Bank plc needs at least £57,000m x 6% = **£4,560m** of Capital to fit the Basel 2 criteria. At least £2,280 (2%) must be Common Equity. Countryside

Bank has capital of £16,500m. It should be noted that these figures are for illustration only.

Thus, it more than covers the Basel 2 requirements but importantly requires only 35% (work it out) of the capital required under Basel 1 to transact the same amount of business. For Countryside this means that its assets can be expanded almost three times based on the same capital position.

It should also be noted that this is a very basic illustration and does not incorporate more sophisticated products and markets that universal and other banks became involved with leading up to 2007.

What is not shown in these figures is the overall cost of compliance – large enough to cause even the biggest banks some concern. Whilst it is a cost of doing business and specialist staff have to be employed and trained to maintain internal guidelines it could steer some institutions towards lower cost domiciles or even changing their business mix.

Basel 3

Basel's response to the global banking crisis was ultimately to call for more capital and for capital "buffers" to cover periods of pro-cyclicality – a phenomenon where capital is stretched as credit growth expands.

Basel 3 also adds sophistication in terms of overall leverage of a bank balance sheet (Tier 1 capital must exceed 3% of average total assets) and in terms of liquidity (holding liquid assets to cover at least 30 days of liquidity requirements).

What is envisaged is a more robust banking system but also one that is more risk averse. The full implications of Basel 3 have yet to be felt. Figure 5.5 compares the key ratios:

Figure 5.5: Key ratios in Basel 1, 2 and 3 compared

	BASEL 1	BASEL 2	BASEL 3
Common equity	n/a	2%	4.5%
Tier 1 (includes above)	4%	4%	6%
Mandatory capital buffer	n/a	n/a	2.5%
Discretionary buffer	n/a	n/a	2.5%
TOTAL	**8%**	**6%**	**10%**

Because such a drastic increase in capital and liquidity requirements cannot be brought in overnight, banks have a phased introduction up to 2018/19 to look forward to.

National regulators have also been busy tightening up the supervisory "pillar" of the accord to focus on other areas of banking risk as shown in the next section.

Banking regulators

In the wake of the global banking crisis some national regulators have been repositioning themselves, not only to reflect the needs of Basel 3 but also to be more effective operationally. The flawed FSA in the UK had its powers taken over (back) by the Bank of England and there now exist new bodies – the Financial Conduct Authority (FCA) alongside the Prudential Regulation Authority (PRA) and the Financial Policy Committee (FPC). These work alongside the Bank of England (responsible also for monetary policy and economic stability) and HM Treasury.

By contrast, in Singapore, a much smaller nation, these functions are undertaken by just one organisation – the Monetary Authority of Singapore (MAS). The MAS is very well respected in its region and offers the following protection to Singapore citizens and its banks:

1. A stable financial SYSTEM
2. Safe & sound INTERMEDIARIES
3. Safe & efficient INFRASTRUCTURE
4. Fair, efficient & transparent MARKETS
5. Transparent & fair-dealing INTERMEDIARIES & OFFERORS
6. Well-informed & empowered CONSUMERS

Many national regulators around the world hold common objectives in respect of their local banking markets. A few of the clearer "mission statements" indicate the common theme of stability:

"to promote sustained non-inflationary economic growth and a sound and progressive financial centre"

MAS, Singapore

"to ensure that the relevant markets function well"

FCA, London

To…."fulfil its (sic) macroeconomic function of efficient and low-cost transformation and provision of financial resources"

Deutsche Bundesbank, Frankfurt

In the Singaporean example the different functions of the MAS are summarised in Figure 5.6. These show where MAS has direct control and where it seeks to influence markets and behaviours.

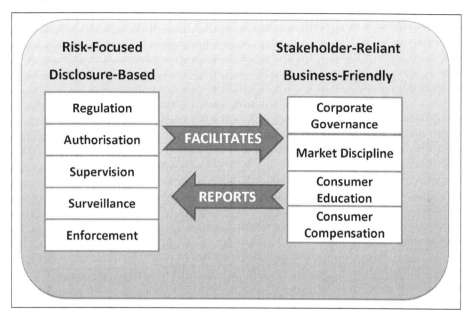

Figure 5.6: Monetary Authority of Singapore functions

Banking risks

Many regulators follow a "risk based" approach to regulation. This recognises risks in two ways. Firstly it recognises that banking encompasses different kinds of risk that could threaten the stability of individual banks and the financial system. It recognises that retail banking customers need more protection, as individuals, than do wholesale banking customers. Secondly it recognises that some risks are more serious than others or more likely to happen and so deploys its resources so that key risks are actively regulated whilst others are monitored.

Banks recognise some key areas of risk as summarised in Figure 5.7:

Figure 5.7: Types of banking risk

Credit Risk	The risk of default and non-performance of assets in the bank balance sheet. For example a loan not being repaid.
Liquidity Risk	The risk that the bank will have insufficient funds or access to funds to meet its obligations to repay deposits or loans (see Chapter 3).
Market Risk	The risk that exposure to particular markets (e.g. property development) will have an adverse effect on a bank. Also covers interest rate risk (see Chapter 3). Markets include interest rate markets, currency markets as well as those in which customers operate.
Operational Risk	The risks relating to physical assets (loss, theft) and the bank's workforce. Included here are risks apparent in payments systems.
Reputational Risk	The risk of poor publicity and the erosion of trust and confidence that this could entail. Almost anything can cause bad publicity – even the announcement of profits (normally the sign of a successful bank).
Legal Risk	The risk that changes in the law could adversely affect a bank's performance and stability. A legal case or appeal could make some contracts void and the bank may be unsecured. Banks can be sued, a factor that can highlight poor bank practices. Other countries' laws can also impact banks where they and their clients operate abroad.

To this list can be added the overall capital risk associated with the lack of capital or over-geared situation and sovereign/political risk, where banks lend to or have assets domiciled in unstable areas of the world.

Clearly it is the interests of banks, themselves, to be aware of these risks and this is why Basel 3, in particular, encourages larger banks to use their own risk assessment systems and for regulators to monitor these rather than impose external systems. It is also felt that the "third pillar" of Basel, the publication of data and information about bank activities, will help the market to regulate itself.

For example, a bank with a poor credit risk assessment history and losses that are written off against shareholders' funds may see a reduction in its own credit rating (from AAA to BBB) which will make loans to the bank more expensive. There is a strong incentive, therefore, for banks to monitor themselves and to have appropriate systems in place to measure or estimate risk.

The tools that the regulators deploy to monitor risks and regulate banks are numerous. They include the following key tools:

- Capital Adequacy – Basel Accords (see above)
- Regular Inspections/Monitoring
- Rules and codes of conduct such as the Banking Conduct of Business Sourcebook
- Complaints/Ombudsman procedure

In the UK the FCA conducts both regular and ad hoc inspections of banks, looking behind the monitoring data to review systems and procedures put in place by the banks themselves. Bank failures such as Barings in 1995 and Johnson Matthey in 1982 were ultimately blamed on management system failures.

The BCOBS is a set of rules governing relationships between banks and their consumer and small business customers, giving detailed rules emanating from the Financial Services and Markets Act, 2000. On 1 April 2013 The FCA took over responsibility for complaints and breaches of the BCOBS provisions. The FCA is said to have more focus and more 'teeth' than its predecessor.

You could, I suppose, wade through the whole of the BCOBS. But what would you learn?

- That 'treating customers fairly' means providing information before, during the currency of and after the sale of a retail banking product.
- That banks must adhere to common law rules (case derived law) on their duties around:
  - providing regular statements
  - not closing an account without 30 days notice (when an account is in credit)
  - the care exercised with customers who are in financial difficulties (here the BCOBS links with the Lending Code).

The BCOBS is not a complete statement of the law and the full legal relationship between banker and customer will still be a good basis for complaints.

The banks in the UK augment this statutory protection for consumers by operating their own code of conduct (The Lending Code). It details the expectations and obligations of savers and borrowers not covered in the BCOBS,

Consumer protection regulation

Lastly in this section the work of the Financial Services Ombudsman is highlighted. There are Ombudsmen or "Complaints men" for different types of financial services including mortgages and loans and insurance. Based in statute they investigate complaints that have become "deadlocked", i.e. have been made through a bank's internal complaints procedure but without a mutually acceptable outcome. The Ombudsman then investigates the complaint and makes a ruling that is binding on the bank (rulings are limited by amount to a maximum of £100,000). Consumers, however, retain the right to take the bank to court if the Ombudsman's ruling does not satisfy them.

So transparency at the level of the individual customer, such as advising the customer of any fees and commissions that the provider will earn based on the customer's choice of product, is essential. This allows customers to make more informed choices about products and compare them with other providers'. This both aids competition and promotes fairness. In the UK a "Retail Distribution Review" highlighted the issue of commissions for financial products subsidising the provision of financial advice. Rules were changed so that advisors must charge separately for advice rather than "hide" commissions.

Certain rules also aim to prevent "insider dealing", where bank staff (or customers) with private information about a company or share issue either buy or sell shares knowing that there will be a share price rise or fall when the news is made public. Although the market is felt to reflect all known information about share prices it can lag behind the "insider".

Fraud or just plain theft is also made more difficult by the vetting of individual staff members in banks and the senior managers of financial services companies. Rights to hold licenses to take deposits or to act as investment advisors are strictly guarded to avoid situations such as the "Barlow Clowes[12]" affair recurring. There will, however, always be risks for the gullible or greedy investor who ignores the maxim:

"If it looks too good to be true, it probably is too good to be true"

Depositors in Icelandic banks and investors in Bernard Madoff's schemes[13] provide recent evidence that common sense is not that common.

Transparency of information can also be at the institutional level as a bank's balance sheet is open to scrutiny by shareholders, customers, analysts and regulators.

Summary

This chapter has covered:
- ▶ The need for regulation
- ▶ Capital adequacy under the Basel Accords

---

12 The Barlow Clowes affair in 1992 was an example of dishonesty by the investment company's chief executive Peter Clowes. Clowes was sentenced to 10 years in prison for his part in the "loss" of investors' funds – a "loss" clearly at odds with the luxury lifestyle that Clowes enjoyed based on his drawings from the company

13 The Madoff scandal is an example of a "Ponzi" scheme, a fraudulent scheme whereby the new investor's funds are used to repay and reward older investors. Increasing funds are needed to keep the "pyramid of lies" intact. Follow this story at http://news.bbc.co.uk/1/hi/business/7977665.stm

▶ Regulation and supervision under national laws
▶ The role and activities of key regulators

Further reading and useful web links

Bank for International Settlements (BIS) website at http://www.bis.org/publ/bcbsca. htm

FCA website at http://www.fca.org.uk

MAS website at http://www.mas.gov.sg

Deutsche Bundesbank website at http://www.bundesbank.de

CHAPTER 6

Competition in Retail Banking

Objectives

After studying this chapter you should be able to:

▶ Outline the frameworks that aid understanding of competition between retail banks.

▶ Explain the key areas of contestability between retail banks.

▶ Describe the key strategies used by retail banks at corporate and market levels.

▶ Discuss the implications of competition for bank stakeholders.

Introduction

Regulation, geography and history will all affect the environment within which retail banks operate. In the UK banks operate on a national level, in the USA state-based banks are more common whilst in Germany the market is structured by regions and bank types (regional co-operative banks have most market share in the consumer and retail sector). In Singapore the market is dominated by three large banks, two international (OCBC and UOB) and one former state bank (DBS). The market is complemented by the Post Office Savings Bank (POSB).

Traditionally, customers would bank locally, visiting the bank branch to transact business but the development of technology means that geography is no such longer a limiting factor.

This chapter offers some basic models of competition that allow us to understand some of the pressures and influences within the operating/market environment of retail banking. The chapter goes on to provide examples of bank strategies that recognise the level of competition faced.

Competition and concentration

One of the biggest drivers of competition in any market is the number of firms operating in that market. In 2010 the Organisation for Economic Co-operation and Development (OECD) found that although there were no links between market concentration (large market shares being dominated by a few large banks) measures taken to remedy the financial crisis may have an impact on competition. As part of its deliberations the OECD estimated market concentration in a number of territories. Some of these data are included in Figure 6.1.

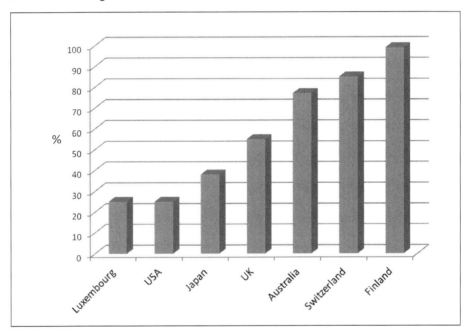

Figure 6.1: Average market share of four largest banks 2000-2007 (OECD)

In the USA there is clear evidence that regulation has effectively prevented bank mergers and acquisitions. Banks, historically, have been state licensed and prevented from operating outside licence areas. This is beginning to be relaxed but the concentration is still at a relatively low level when compared with many other developed nations.

In Finland, as in much of Scandinavia, the market is dominated by Nordea. Nordea emerged as the result of the Swedish banking crisis in 1991. After its forerunner Nordbanken was rescued by the Swedish government it was privatised and began a series of mergers across Denmark, Sweden, Norway and Finland. This was allowed by competition authorities who feared a repeat of the banking crisis that decimated many smaller banks.

The implications of market concentration, however, are monitored closely by competition authorities worldwide. In the EU and USA legal restrictions can be placed on banks that grow and exceed certain market share limits (typically 25%). This has given rise in the UK to the sale of "excess branches" by Lloyds Banking Group and Royal Bank of Scotland following mergers at the start of the financial crisis.

Where a small number of large banks dominate the market they can be part of a powerful oligopoly. This text cannot offer a full description of these complex economic concepts but three brief illustrations will help to understand:

a) Interchange fees for plastic cards

There are, globally, two major card scheme providers that many banks are affiliated to: MasterCard and Visa (see also Chapter 10). One of the ways in which banks profit from issuing cards and "acquiring" retailers/merchants to accept cards is via the "interchange fee". The fee is paid by the merchant's bank to the cardholder's bank to compensate for the risks and costs it incurs in processing the payment request. It is recouped by the merchant's bank by charging the merchant a fee based on the type and value of the transaction processed.

Thus, there are two card schemes that have the opportunity to fix prices or to influence them heavily in a way that would subvert open competition. The implication of this is that charges to merchants and thus prices for consumers are being kept artificially high and that MasterCard and Visa are competing unfairly.

The practice is the subject of an Office of Fair Trading investigation due to report in 2014. It must be stressed that there is no evidence currently in the public domain that gives an indication one way or the other.

Heavy fines are the likely outcome if the card schemes are found guilty.

b) Rigging LIBOR

Already noted in Chapter 2 this is the scandal that has enveloped UK and US banks. The London InterBank Offered Rate (LIBOR) is the rate of interest agreed via the British Bankers' Association (BBA) each day that banks use to benchmark loan interest rates and to lend to each other on the interbank market.

A small number of London banks quote a range of dealing rates to the BBA at a specified time each day. The BBA calculates an average rate, based on a predetermined mechanism, and publishes this as the LIBOR for that day.

During the financial crisis of 2007-2008 some London-based banks sought to "rig" the LIBOR by colluding to quote erroneous rates to the BBA so that

LIBOR was higher or lower than the real market rate. A higher rate allowed banks to charge more for LIBOR linked loans. Lower rates paid by banks made them look more creditworthy than they really were.

Heavy fines exceeding £2billion have already been levied.

These examples illustrate that illegal collusion and price fixing are possible where certain market conditions exist:

▷ A small number of large banks dominate the industry
▷ The products of the banks are homogenous or differentiated only by branding
▷ Banks have formal and informal mechanisms for signalling prices/interest rates to each other
▷ Banks can effectively keep new entrants out of the industry or market
▷ The product/service offered is an economic necessity good – consumers have a high demand for it
▷ The market is mature – growth in market share comes from consumer switching rather than from market growth.

But not every oligopoly gives rise to illegal collusion or the threat of OFT investigation. Markets with the above features can exist in a state of interdependence as illustrated in the third illustration.

c) Why are house mortgage rates offered by different banks so similar?

Look on any price comparison website and the similarity between house mortgage rates is striking. At the time of writing this book Google Compare offers rates for two year fixed mortgages in England as follows:

Skipton Building Society	1.78%
Chelsea Building Society	1.64%
Nationwide Building Society	1.84%
Santander	1.89%

Not only does this market in the UK bear all of the features listed above but changes in rates are also of a similar size and in a similar direction. Why?

There is logic to this and it goes something like this: All mortgage lenders have the same basic costs to cover (Rates paid to savers for example) and so when savings rates change, rates offered to borrowers change to reflect the change in costs.

In addition, each lender sets its rate based not only on costs and perceived risk but also with an eye on competitors' rates. Rate movements are, therefore, interdependent. It may look collusive but there is plenty of evidence to suggest that this is simply the oligopolistic market working.

The scope of competition

In order to analyse the ways in which competition affects the markets in which retail banks operate the "five forces" model devised by Michael Porter of Harvard Business School will be used. Porter's model combines a number of micro-economic and strategic ideas and has its strength in having been built using observations of actual behaviour. Figure 6.2 summarises the basic model:

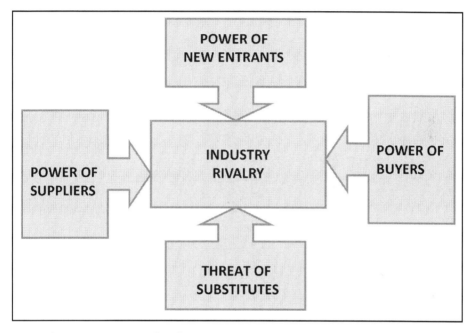

Figure 6.2: Porter's five forces model of competition

The model considers a market (not an individual bank) and the five forces that can influence the type of competition faced by incumbent operators. At this point we must recognise that retail banks operate in a number of different markets with different features and different competitors. Although these are detailed later in the book it is necessary at this stage to focus on examples of markets such as consumer credit, payments, SME accounts, and lending and insurance. The five forces impacting on markets to a greater or lesser extent relate to.

The bargaining power of suppliers

This relates to the power held by suppliers (lenders, depositors and shareholders) to the market competitors to influence the level of competition. This will depend on the number of suppliers, the nature of the "supplies" they offer and the costs of switching to new ones. Since the lifeblood of a bank is liquidity the work of liability managers needs to ensure that no one source of funding is allowed to influence bank decision making too greatly. The sorry tale of Northern Rock's reliance on market funding to fuel its rapid market expansion in House Mortgages is an example of supplier power.

Supplier power may also be influenced by the threat of market entry by the supplier itself. An insurer, for example, could invest in starting its own bank, rather than buying the bonds of existing competitors. This is exactly what happened in 1998 in the UK market when Egg bank arrived on the scene as a subsidiary of Prudential Insurance. Interestingly, the ability of a government majority shareholder to influence behaviour in the SME lending market in the UK has not been marked.

Bargaining power of buyers

Customers are an important ingredient in competition and can influence this if they have bargaining leverage by being concentrated or buying in volume as they can favour one competitor over another. The better the information about rivals in the market and the lower the costs of switching from one seller to another; the more ready a buyer can be to transfer allegiance. Individual customers have little bargaining power and are often reluctant to switch to another bank as this could have a negative impact on regular payments and on a credit score. In the UK a guaranteed switching service came into operation in 2013 to try to free up movement. In addition Price Comparison websites do give some power to buyers as they provide more information about specific products and services than most customers can obtain by themselves.

Threats from new entrants

Some financial services markets are easier to enter due to their low capital requirements and lower skill needs whilst others are protected through domination by large firms, cost and branding advantages of existing banks as well as regulation and a high dependence on technology. Markets that are easy to enter are likely to be more competitive whilst others can be monopolistic. Retail banking markets such as payments markets can be threatened by new entrants (see Chapters 9 and 10) who specialise in one aspect of the business.

Threats from substitutes

Where consumers can find alternatives to the output of a particular market they may use the alternatives where the relative price performance is better and the costs of switching are lower. For a provider of retail banking services the strength of this threat is diminished by the very advantages that financial intermediation brings. Elsewhere in this book, however, the threat of Peer to Peer (P2P) lenders, internet only banks, non-bank payment services etc. are all described. Thus, a retail bank must compete not only with other banks but also with customers deciding not to use banks at all.

Finally, rivalry amongst existing competitors

This focuses on the type of competition that the market generates – cost led or product differentiation. It will also be influenced by the number of market participants, growth in the market and the level of costs of getting out of the market if profits fail. Where competitiveness relies on low prices, as seems to be the case with house insurance, for example, the firm must be able to sustain this via lower costs and efficiencies. Larger firms with greater financial reserves can keep prices low until rivals have left the market.

By this feature of the model we can see that retail banks around the world consider that there is strong rivalry within their markets. The levels of corporate and market specific advertising and sponsorship show that maintaining strong brand awareness is important. International travellers will be well aware of the branding of air-bridges in many airports by HSBC. Football fans will also note the series of sponsors entertained by Newcastle United (Northern Rock, Virgin Money and Wonga) whilst Manchester United has had AIG and AON and Liverpool, Standard Chartered.

Retail bank strategies

There are examples and illustrations throughout this book of the various strategies used by retail banks to compete in the various markets served by them.

Retail banks have a number of stakeholders – people and organisations for whom the successful running of a bank is essential:

- Shareholders – who are interested in returns on their investment
- Consumers – who are interested in good service and in choice and convenience but at low cost to them
- Managers and Employees – who are interested in career progression, pay and, often, a sense of achievement and professionalism
- The Government – who are interested in a well-functioning banking system as an engine for economic growth and a bastion of economic stability.

What binds each stakeholder together is one key metric – profitability. Profits are a signal of success and stability in the market; give better returns to shareholders, better rewards to staff and, potentially; more investment in better services to consumers (that last one is a bit of a stretch).

Retail bank strategies are seen in the context of long term and stable profits and also in the context of the global environment (Chapter 1); the risk factors inherent in banking (Chapters 2 and 3) and the regulatory environment (Chapters 4 and 5). Strategies include:

Corporate level strategies

i. Branding – brand and image awareness are important in retaining customers and engendering trust.

ii. Funding strategies – Asset and Liability Management.

iii. Operational Efficiencies – Covered in Chapters 9 and 10 relating to delivery systems and payments and also Chapter 11 on lending. Strategies can include out-sourcing of functions, use of overseas or remote call centres and automation of payments.

iv. Portfolio strategies – decisions on which markets to focus on and which to exit. Banks can capitalise on key skills and expertise and function only in markets where these add value.

v. Growth strategies – domestic and international.

Market level strategies

vi. Product design – this acknowledges both innovation and knowledge of markets and competitors.

vii. Pricing strategies – again, acknowledging competition but also controlling margins and risks.

viii. Product advertising – Corporate sponsorship is focused on branding but individual adverts can focus on details of products and comparisons with others.

ix. Delivery strategies – dealt with more fully in Chapter 9.

x. Partnership strategies – In Chapters 9 and 10 we see how certain banking systems require co-operation to work efficiently and effectively.

Summary

This chapter has covered:
- ▶ Frameworks that aid understanding of competition between retail banks.
- ▶ The key areas of contestability between retail banks
- ▶ Key strategies used by retail banks at corporate and market levels.
- ▶ Implications of competition for bank stakeholders.

Further Reading and useful web links

Porter, ME, (2008), The Five Competitive Forces That Shape Strategy, *Harvard Business Review*, January 2008.

OECD, (2010), Competition, Concentration and Stability in the Banking Sector, [online]: http://www.oecd.org/regreform/sectors/46040053.pdf

Section B

CHAPTER 7

The Banker-Customer Relationship

Objectives

After studying this chapter you should be able to:

▶ Outline the legal/contractual relationship between banks and their customers

▶ Recognise the importance of trust in the banker/customer relationship

▶ Describe the typical obligations and rights of the debtor/creditor relationship

▶ Explain the concept of "Treating Customers Fairly"

▶ Explain the various legal relationships that underpin banking products and services.

Introduction

The subject of the banker/customer contract is potentially huge and can become mired in detailed legal issues that the retail banker can (and perhaps should) outsource to the bank's legal department. This is further complicated by the fact that major and minor legal and practical differences exist between different countries. European Union countries retain historical differences that will affect the contractual relationship, the remedies when things go wrong and the behaviour of banks within the relationship.

This part of the text, therefore, provides an overview of key banking relationship issues from a practical perspective and focuses on the clear principles that bankers should adhere to rather than on the detail of the law. National differences are highlighted but reference to UK law and practice is prevalent as they do reflect and influence the legal regimes in large parts of the English-speaking world.

In this first chapter of section B of the text the basic contract between the banker and the customer is reviewed. Once again there is a need to look back into history to see how and why the different rules that form the legal environment for bank operations have come about.

Practical and commercial considerations are also studied as well as other legal relationships that underpin bank products and services.

One key duty of the bank is that of secrecy. In Chapter 2 we saw that bankers need to keep their customers' affairs secret in order to create an environment of trust, necessary for their activities as intermediaries. In some legal systems (e.g. Switzerland) the duty of secrecy is supported by statute law and only in recent years have exceptions to the rule been allowed so that drug money and terrorist financing can be revealed. This chapter covers the banker's general duty of secrecy and reveals that it has many holes.

Sources of UK law relating to retail banking

This text identifies THREE key sources of legal rules:
1. Acts of Parliament/Regulation
2. Case Law, via the civil courts, and
3. Custom and Usage.

Statute law includes specific Acts relating to banking, such as The Cheques Acts 1957 and 1992 as well as more general ones such as The Proceeds of Crime Act 2002, The Data Protection Act 1998 and the Supply of Goods and Services Act 1982. It also includes rules generated by statutory bodies such as the Financial Conduct Authority (FCA) and Prudential Regulation Authority (PRA).

Case law is generated via specific individual cases being decided in the courts (sometimes at appeal). The importance of a case depends mainly on the status of the court where the case was heard. The senior UK court is the Supreme Court, whose decisions are binding on all courts in the UK and create precedents that must be followed.

Acts of Parliament can overrule any decision of any English Court and European Community law often binds UK lawmakers too as do decisions of the European Court of Human Rights.

In case law the date of a case is also quite important as cases often interpret statutes in particular situations. Over time these situations can change. For example a case decided on the duties of a bank in 1890 and relying on the phrase "normal business hours" (Bills of Exchange Act 1882) would limit the hours to weekdays between 9.30 a.m. and 3.30 p.m. In 2013 it would have to take into consideration Saturday opening and 24-hour banking. However, the principle that the bank owed a duty under the Act would remain the same.

The final source of law is **Custom and Usage**. Banks abide not only by regulatory rules but also by the norms of commercial practice. Over time custom and usage become either common law via cases or statute law. The Bills of Exchange Act 1882 (see Chapter 10) is an excellent Act that is still in force today but really only codified what banks and their customers were already doing.

Before leaving this section it should be pointed out that many key areas of modern retail banking activity are not covered by specific statute law but rely on a mixture of statutes and cases that govern contract law. Figure 7.1 provides a timeline of developments in the UK with specific reference to payment transactions.

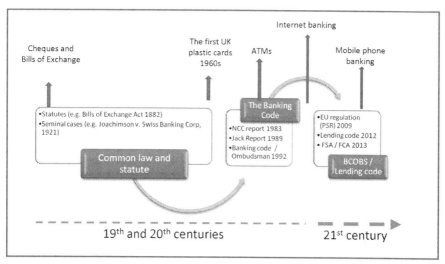

Figure 7.1   A timeline of developments in UK banking law

The banker-customer relationship

The main relationship between a bank and its customer is that of debtor and creditor. A customer who has deposited money (the creditor) is owed money by the bank (the debtor). A customer (the debtor) who has borrowed money from the bank owes money to the bank (the creditor). The relationship is the same even though the roles can switch from time to time.

In the legal case *Foley v Hill* (1848), the customer argued that the relationship was different – the bank was a trustee of the money which he had deposited and that he therefore had a right to share in the profits (trustees have special duties to the people for whom they act as trustees). It was held that there was no element of trusteeship, the relationship being merely that of debtor and creditor – after all, intermediation and credit creation would fail if banks merely held money in trust and could not lend it.

However, there is something unusual about this relationship because the general practice is that the debtor has a duty to seek out and repay his creditors. This does not apply to banks who are debtors, i.e. have had money deposited with them. Think about it for a minute – banks couldn't continue in business if they had to write to every customer with a current account in credit every January, asking every one of them if they would like their money back!

This point was central to understanding the seminal case in this area: *Joachimsson v Swiss Bank Corporation* (1921). In this case Joachimsson was unable to obtain his assets during the First World War as he left the UK as an "enemy alien". He sued the bank after the war for the return of his money. The Court of Appeal highlighted the need for a customer to demand repayment of their money before the bank would have a duty to repay. Until the demand, the money was owned by the bank.

Remember, please, that this unusual aspect of the relationship does not apply if the bank is the creditor (the lender). Unless the borrowing is taken by way of a loan account, the borrowing customer should seek out his creditor (the bank).

The judge in this case also went on to describe other aspects of the debtor-creditor relationship where the bank is debtor. Thus, just as it is impractical to expect banks to seek out their depositors (creditors) so it is unreasonable for customers to demand payment at any branch or at any time. Demand must be made by the customer:

- In writing
- During normal banking hours
- At the branch where the account is maintained or at a mutually agreed branch.

These are important details. Demand must be made by the *customer*, therefore signatures authorising withdrawals must be genuine or third parties demanding money must be appropriately authorised by the customer.

A bank's obligations to its customers

Based on the judgment laid down by Atkin LJ in the Joachimsson case in 1921 and subsequent cases and statutes we can piece together an inventory of the key duties owed by a bank to its customers:

1. To honour its customer's cheques to the credit balance on the account or to the agreed overdraft limit, provided:
    a) the cheques are properly drawn and they have not been countermanded (stopped);
    b) there are no legal bars to prevent funds being paid to third parties, such as bankruptcy orders or orders of court.
2. To maintain strict secrecy about customers' affairs, subject to certain exceptions (see below).

3. To follow its usual course of business and to be consistent.

4. To give reasonable notice to a customer when closing an account in credit. In *Prosperity Ltd v Lloyds Bank* (1923), Prosperity Ltd. was selling insurance and had printed and distributed prospectuses stating (correctly) that the bank had agreed to accept applications. The scheme was heavily criticised in the press as a fraud and the bank then wished to close the account and minimise the bad publicity. It gave Prosperity one month to close the account, which was in credit. Prosperity sued for breach of contract. The bank was held to be in breach of contract because one month's notice was insufficient, given the complex arrangements made with it for the receipt of applications.

5. To provide a statement of account within a reasonable time and a statement of the balance on request. Note here that the customer has no obligation to read the statement.

6. Moreover the bank must keep accurate records. If it wrongly advises a customer of a credit to his or her account then the customer can retain the excess credit if:
   a) the bank misrepresented the account to the customer;
   b) the customer was misled by the inaccurate information and used the funds as a result; and
   c) the customer's position had changed, so that it would be unfair for the customer to repay the money.

United Overseas Bank v Jiwani (1976) is a good example of these rules. Jiwani's account was credited with US$11,000 by telex: whereupon he spent the proceeds of the credit as part payment for a hotel. Later, the bank received a confirmation of the telex message and mistakenly advised Jiwani of a further credit of US$11,000, which he again spent. The bank sued Jiwani for the return of the second credit. It was held that, while the first two rules applied, the bank had misrepresented the account to the customer, who was misled by this into using the funds as a result of the misrepresentation and so the third rule did not. Because Jiwani had other funds which he could have used to finance the second transaction, it would therefore be fair for Jiwani to repay the money.

7. To receive a customer's money and cheques for collection and to credit his account with them.

8. To repay credit balances on a current account on demand but only:
   a) at the customer's written request;
   b) during banking hours; and
   c) at the branch where the account is maintained or at another mutually agreed branch.

9. To advise the customer immediately if and when forgery is brought to the bank's attention. In *Brown v Westminster Bank* (1964), over 100 forged cheques had been paid by the bank but on several occasions the bank had queried the cheques with the customer, who had told it that the signatures were genuine. In fact, the cheques had been forged by Brown's wife. When she died, Brown sued the bank for negligence in paying forged cheques. It was held that, having maintained that the cheques were not forgeries, Brown could not now claim that they were forgeries and so lost his action. Preventing somebody from 'changing his tune' is an example of the legal principle of estoppel – Brown was estopped from denying that the cheques were forgeries because of his previous words and actions.

10. To exercise proper care and diligence, especially with regard to the payment and collection of cheques under the Bills of Exchange Act 1882 and the Cheques Act 1957 (see Chapter 10).

This particular section may appear complex and laboured but it is important to identify the normal expectations of the relationship as this will inform bank behaviour, underpin formal, written contracts such as plastic card contracts, and serve as a basis for decisions about complaints.

The duty of secrecy

The leading case is *Tournier v National Provincial and Union Bank* (1924). Tournier was employed on a quarterly contract. He was a gambler and had overdrawn his account and failed to keep up the repayments agreed with the bank. The bank phoned him at his office but he was out. The bank then informed Tournier's employer of his gambling and debt to the bank, and the employer, as a result, did not renew Tournier's contract of employment. Tournier sued the bank for breach of contract and won. It was held that the disclosure of his affairs was a breach of contract because it could not be justified under any of four headings. These four exceptions to the duty of secrecy are:

- Compulsion of law
- Public interest
- Interests of the bank, and
- Customer authority

The following sections deal with each exception in turn.

A bank can be compelled to disclose the customer's affairs by reason of an Act of Parliament. One example is the Taxes Management Act 1970 which compels banks to notify HM Customs and Revenue of customers whose accounts are credited with interest above certain amount.

More recent Acts of Parliament to combat *money laundering*[14] through banks share certain concepts of enforcement that affect the bank's duty of secrecy.

The key legislation here is the Proceeds of Crime Act 2002. It follows legislation on terrorism and drug trafficking which have similar features:

▶ A banker must disclose suspicions about customers' transactions to the relevant authorities, the National Criminal Intelligence Service (NCIS). These suspicions must have arisen in the ordinary course of business, they must be reasonable suspicions or actual knowledge and they must be disclosed as soon as practicable (section 330).

▶ It is an offence to tip off the suspect that a disclosure has been made (section 333).

The second exception relates to a duty of **disclosure to the public**, where such a disclosure would be in the public interest. The Jack Committee in 1989 regarded this exception to the duty of secrecy as being of minimal importance, in view of the many Acts it quoted requiring disclosure of a customer's affairs, nearly all of which had been passed by Parliament since 1924. However, the duty still remains in relation to trading with enemy aliens in time of war.

The third exception is when it is in the **bank's interest** to disclose the customer's affairs. Thus, when a bank wishes to sue a customer for an unpaid debt it must disclose the balance of the account when engaging debt collectors or when applying to court. Another instance might be making enquiries of a customer's relatives or doctor if mental incapacity is suspected. A more common example is the practice of sharing information on credit default and credit requests with other banks via *credit reference agencies*. In addition, banks now pass names and addresses of customers to their subsidiary companies, enabling them to sell other financial services by means of direct mail shots to the customers' homes.

Finally when **the customer has given express or implied consent**, the bank may disclose information to third parties. Express written or verbal consent will always be requested for bankers' references as the bankers traditional use of "implied consent" was tested in *Turner v Royal Bank of Scotland* (1999). RBS had relied on implied consent but Turner had objected to a reference being sent. The court held that even though the practice was common amongst banks that was insufficient to bind customers as it "did not amount to usage". In addition it was a breach of the Banking Code. The Turner case became one of the first legal tests of the code.

Implied consent problems arise in many routine banking functions such as the collection of bank statements from a branch by a company employee or a friend or

---

14 Money Laundering is a term that describes the "washing" of proceeds of crime through legitimate financial services so that its original source is hidden. Terrorist organisations, drugs traffickers and criminals (including tax avoiders) may use legitimate bank accounts to effect transfers of funds, investments and take loans in order to mask criminal activity. The opening of accounts is also affected by Money Laundering Regulations

parent accompanying a customer to an interview. In these cases banks will seek express consent, preferably in writing, to avoid any confusion.

Problems may also arise with a new practice – the sale for cash of parcels of loans from one bank/mortgage lender to another (securitisation). If the selling bank discloses to the buyer information about the borrowers, then it may breach its duty of confidentiality, unless the borrowers have already given their consent in the loan agreements.

Telephone or direct banking brings its own problems too. Identification of customers calling the direct bank is of paramount importance and elaborate systems of passwords and codes are set up with the customer at the outset to prevent bank staff discussing personal financial affairs with unauthorised people.

One final note relates to the Data Protection Act 1998. Under this Act it is an offence by a bank to disclose any information about a customer without the consent of the customer. Thus by making an unauthorised disclosure a bank may be liable to damages for breach of contract and a fine from the Data Protection Registrar.

A bank's duty of care when giving advice

A bank has an overriding duty of care to its customers especially when giving advice to them. *Spindler & Verity v Lloyds Bank plc* (1995) highlights the dangers inherent in not observing this implied contract term.

After discussions between Mr Spindler and Miss Verity and a local branch manager, Lloyds Bank agreed to lend the couple £152,000 to cover the purchase and renovation costs of a house. Spindler and Verity purchased the property for £126,500, with a view to renovating it and then selling at a profit. The property market was booming and the constant increase in house prices gave all concerned a false sense of confidence. Unfortunately the proposition did not work out as anticipated because property market prices began to fall, the cost of the renovation (£26,000) exceeded the original estimate by £16,000, and interest rates began to rise.

Spindler and Verity sold the property in May 1990 for £135,000 at a time when the amount owing to the bank had risen to £208,000 due to interest costs.

Lloyds pursued the couple for repayment of the shortfall but Spindler and Verity instigated proceedings against the bank claiming:

▶ Lloyds had acted negligently in advancing the £152,000.
▶ The couple had suffered emotional distress and loss of earnings.
▶ The couple had lost money on the forced sale of another property which had to be sold to help to meet the obligations to Lloyds on the loan in question.

The court ruled that under ordinary circumstances there is no duty for the bank to give advice upholding the existing law following *Redmond v Allied Irish Banks* (1987).

However, when a customer asks for advice and the bank is aware, or ought to be aware, that the customer is relying on that advice, then a duty of care will arise.

The ruling was based on the fact that had the local manager exercised reasonable care and skill he would have told Spindler and Verity that the whole project was too risky and that they should forget about it. Lloyds' counter argument that Spindler and Verity had not relied on this advice but had made up their own minds about the project was fatally damaged when Lloyds' own "Starting Your Business" leaflet was examined. The leaflet said that "Your bank manager will help you decide how much you can really afford to invest" and "Do not hesitate to ask your manager for advice".

Damages awarded against the bank, because the loss arose as a result of the bank's negligent advice, were calculated as if the transaction had never taken place. The court declined to award damages for emotional distress and adjourned the hearing on the loss of earnings suffered. It is believed that Lloyds settled this latter claim out of court.

The banker's customer

So far this text has not differentiated between types of customer – but the law does and banks must be aware that customers come in a variety of legal guises as described in Figure 7.2.

Key for the bank is identifying to whom obligations are owed under the contract and from whom repayment of debts can be demanded.

Figure 7.2: Types of customer and account liability

CUSTOMER TYPE	KEY FEATURES	ACCOUNT LIABILITY
Sole Account	Personal account with one account holder. Others may be allowed to sign on the account	Sole account holder
Joint Account	Personal account where two or more people share the account.	Both account holders individually and jointly
Minors	Personal account holders under 18.	The account holder or a guarantor, depending on circumstances
Sole Trader	Business account. Others may be allowed to sign on the account.	Sole trader
Partnership	Business where two or more people join together to run a business with a view to profit.	The partners individually and together

CUSTOMER TYPE	KEY FEATURES	ACCOUNT LIABILITY
Limited Liability Partnership	LLPs are professional or trading businesses where partners have limited their liability.	*The partners, individually and together up to a limit.*
Companies	Incorporated limited companies owned by shareholders. They have a separate legal identity to their owners and managers.	*The company*
Trustees	Business or personal account where funds belonging to a third party are held "in Trust" for a beneficiary.	*The beneficial owner of the funds unless the trustee acts outside their powers*
Clubs and Societies	Unincorporated bodies run by a committee.	*The committee members*

Customers' obligations to a bank

There are two parties to the banker-customer contract and duties under the contract run both ways. Banks have rights against the customer where they do not fulfil their duties correctly.

The key duties are:

1. To take reasonable care when writing cheques (technically termed drawing cheques) so as to prevent fraud or forgery, and also not to mislead the bank. In *London Joint Bank v Macmillan & Arthur* (1918), a bearer cheque payable to the account-holding firm (M&A) had been drawn by one of its clerks for '£2', but with no amount expressed in words, and signed by a partner. The clerk who had written the cheque then altered the '£2' to '£120' and wrote in the amount as 'One hundred and twenty pounds'. Since the box for the figures originally appeared as '£2', the change to '£120' was therefore simple. The firm sued the bank but lost because it had not exercised sufficient care when drawing and signing the cheque.

2. To advise the bank immediately it is discovered that cheques are being forged. In *Greenwood v Martins Bank* (1932) the customer delayed notifying the bank for eight months and was held to be in breach of his duty to inform the bank immediately the forgeries were discovered.

3. To demand repayment of a credit balance, the customer must go to the branch of the bank where the account is maintained, in business hours, and make a demand in writing. The bank does not have to seek out its creditors.

4. Before signing a cheque, the customer must ensure that the account has sufficient funds or sufficient leeway in the overdraft limit to meet the cheque.
5. To repay an overdraft on demand (*Williams & Glyns Bank v Brown* (1980)).
6. To pay reasonable interest and commission and to reimburse the bank for any costs or losses from operating the account (Supply of Goods and Services Act 1982).

In Chapter 10 we review payments systems and note the increase in use of plastic cards, mobile payments and internet transactions. Whilst protections and security measures exist it is important to note that customer obligations to banks and card issuers under written contracts mirror the older case law. For example, when using a plastic card, which is always the property of the bank and the loss of which must be reported immediately (point 2 above), the customer has a duty to exercise care, as laid down in the card's conditions of use. In particular, the PIN (personal identification number) must not be written down anywhere. This mirrors the duty outlined at Point 1 above.

Treating Customers Fairly (TCF)

The Banking Conduct of Business Sourcebook (BCOBS), published by the FCA is a set of rules governing relationships between banks and their consumer and small business customers, giving detailed rules emanating from the Financial Services and Markets Act, 2000. On 1 April 2013 The Financial Conduct Authority (FCA), took over responsibility for complaints and breaches of the BCOBS provisions. The FCA is said to have more focus and more 'teeth' than its predecessor.

You could, I suppose, wade through the whole of the BCOBS or even the marginally more user-friendly industry guidance from the BBA (BBA, 2011). But what would you learn?

▶ That 'treating customers fairly' means providing information before, during the currency of and after the sale of a retail banking product.
▶ That banks must adhere to common law rules (case derived law) on their duties around:
  ▶ providing regular statements
  ▶ not closing an account without 30 days' notice (when an account is in credit)
  ▶ the care exercised with customers who are in financial difficulties (here the BCOBS links with the Lending Code).

The BCOBS is not a complete statement of the law and the full legal relationship between banker and customer will still be a good basis for complaints. Where the BCOBS is silent, of course, is on the obligations and duties of customers regarding notification of lost or compromised PINs, forged cheques and signatures, mistaken payments etc. These matters are dealt with via individual terms and conditions relating to a specific product.

The Lending Code

From 1992 many UK banks entered into a voluntary code, the Banking Code, as a basis for the "contract" between a bank and its personal customers. Updated and revised every three to four years the Code improved customer awareness of bank practice and has given additional protection.

The Code also gave customers a proper basis for complaints and is seen to be speedier to react to consumer concerns than the law.

The Banking Code covers the following areas:
- Ten key commitments to ensure fairness and openness
- Information about products and services
- Advice of interest rates and changes
- Bank charges (including cash machine charges)
- Running and changing accounts
- Protection such as secrecy and PIN security
- Financial difficulties and complaints

The BCOBS, however, together other regulatory instruments, has removed certain parts of the code which were by then on a statutory footing (see Figure 7.1) and in 2012 the British Bankers Association (BBA) replaced it with a shorter "Lending Code" covering the areas not affected by statute.

The Lending Code concerns itself with credit decisions and credit default and echoes a number of the key BCOBS concepts regarding provision of information before, during and after the sale of a credit product. The code (like the BCOBS) is limited to consumers and business customers with turnover below £1million – micro-enterprises. What is also important is that the code is voluntary – the last remaining element of self-regulation but covering, arguably, the most contentious part of bank activity – credit granting.

The minimum standards expected relate to 'information giving that is complete, clear and timely and that customers are to be treated fairly'. The Lending Code attempts to outline the credit environment within which banks work, bringing customers' attention to the following (not an exhaustive list):
- Use of credit reference agencies (even a declined application can be recorded as a credit event). Here banks want to protect themselves and customers from over-extending credit as they share details of other facilities held with other institutions.

▶ The information needs for proper credit decisions to be made, including the recommendation of independent (legal) advice before committing, facility letters, how long the credit decision process will take and the ban on unlimited personal guarantees.

▶ The fact that Terms and Conditions need to be drawn to the customer's attention before purchase, if possible.

▶ Being 'sympathetic and positive' in cases of financial difficulties and listening to realistic repayment proposals. Banks must vet debt collection companies scrupulously before selling them debt assets.

▶ Providing a clear complaints procedure.

Other relationships between banks and customers

Not every interaction between a bank and its customers falls under the debtor-creditor relationship discussed above. Other legal relationships, bearing different duties and rights, exist depending on the nature of the transaction. The most common relationships are:

▶ **Principal and Agent:** Where a bank acts on a customer's instruction (payment of a cheque to a third party, purchase or sale of stocks and shares or arrangement of an insurance policy with a third party company). In this relationship some basic rules apply such as carrying out the customer's instruction without negligence and not making secret profits – so all potential commissions payable must be disclosed to the customer.

▶ **Bailor and Bailee:** These two archaic terms refer to the contract of bailment, which arises when property is lodged by the bailor with the bailee for specific purpose, e.g. repair of a motor car or the cleaning of a suit or dress. In banking, the deposit of deeds or securities for safe custody at a branch is an example of bailment. The customer is the bailor, the bank is the bailee. A paid bailee, known as a bailee for reward, owes a greater degree of care to the bailor than does an unpaid or gratuitous bailee. The paid bailee must exercise the greatest degree of care that people might reasonably expect from a person in that type of business. The duty of an unpaid bailee is to care for the property in the same way as a reasonably prudent and careful person would look after their own property of a similar type. As banks typically charge for this service they are generally expected to achieve the higher level of care of the bailee for reward.

▶ **Mortgagor/Mortgagee:** Here the mortgagor (customer) has mortgaged his or her property to the bank (mortgagee) as security for a loan or overdraft.

The law gives each party certain rights and duties. The property mortgaged is usually land (houses) but can be stocks and shares.

▶ **Trustee/constructive trustee:** This is a rare relationship but one that can arise where a bank knows, or should have known, that funds held in a bank account should not be used for a specific purpose yet allows them to be so used. An example of this comes in *Barclays Bank Ltd v Quistclose Investments Ltd.* (1970). In this case the bank was aware that certain funds in the troubled company's account should only be used for a specific purpose. Instead the bank allowed the funds to be drawn against ordinary expenses. The bank was in breach of trust and had to repay funds from its own resources. In *Lipkin Gorman v Karpnale* (1989), however, the bank had to be knowingly dishonest to be in breach of constructive trust when dealing with withdrawals from an account.

Summary

This chapter has covered:

▶ The legal/contractual relationship between banks and their customers under UK law

▶ The typical obligations and rights of the debtor/creditor relationship

▶ The concept of "Treating Customers Fairly"

▶ The various legal relationships that underpin banking products and services.

Further reading

BBA (2012) The Lending Code [online]. Available at: http://www.bba.org.uk/media/article/the-lending-code.

BBA (2011) Industry guidance for FSA Banking Conduct of Business Sourcebook [online]. Available at: http://www.bba.org.uk/media/article/industry-guidance-for-fsa-banking-conduct-of-business-sourcebook

Financial Conduct Authority, (2013) Banking: Conduct of Business Sourcebook [online], http://www.fca.org.uk/your-fca/documents/handbook-releases/handbook-release-136-release-files-business-standards

Prudential Regulation Authority Handbook, (2013) http://www.fshandbook.info/FS/html/PRA

Roberts G, (2013), *Law Relating to Financial Services*, 8th edn., Global Professional Publishing.

CHAPTER 8

Retail Banking Products

Objectives

After studying this chapter you should be able to:

▸ Describe the various types of account and facility that banks may offer

▸ Explain the differences between bank account types

▸ Outline the non-interest-based products and services offered by banks

▸ Explain the importance of interest and non-interest revenues to retail banks.

Introduction

We saw in Chapter 3 that retail banks work and make profit in two main ways: interest- and non-interest-based products. Interest-based products are the traditional offerings of retail banks and net interest spread (the difference between interest paid to lenders (depositors) and interest charged to borrowers) is a key source of profit.

Modern retail banks are also in a prime position to offer associated financial products both to lenders and borrowers and to the general population. These products are commission or fee based, adding to bank profits in a way that is unaffected by movements in interest rates. Products such as insurance, pensions and investments fall into this category.

This chapter reviews the different types of basic bank account both for savers and borrowers. It is important to note that their provision often fulfil basic economic and lifestyle needs. The chapter also looks at non-interest-based products and the specific risks they introduce.

Types of savings account

The types of account offered in the retail banking market are listed at Figure 8.1. The provision of such products really defines a retail bank. We now explore different account types to see how they work and how the bank might deploy them to best suit the needs of customers.

These basic accounts provide some basic features relating to the functions of money for all depositors as they offer easy access, a store of value and a medium of exchange. Due to the ability to transfer funds between accounts and access them using cheques, debit cards, ATMs, the internet or even mobile phones, depositors do not have to go to the bank to withdraw their funds in cash in order to use them to make purchases. In this way money held in bank accounts is a vital part of the supply of money.

Figure 8.1: Types of savings account

Current account	*Basic account with cheque book and debit card facility. Pays a very small amount of interest (or none at all). Interest is often foregone in exchange for "free" banking – where transactions attract no fee for the customer.*
Deposit account	*Cash savings that pay interest at regular intervals. Often these are protected by notice periods such as seven days.*
Individual savings account (ISA)	*Tax free interest on cash savings up to a limit in each tax year.*
Term savings	*Longer term cash savings often with restricted access (longer notice periods) and higher interest rates.*

Individual depositors also have different motivations for saving and as intermediaries it is necessary for retail banks to understand these in order to garner sufficient deposits to undertake lending business.

Future expenditure

There is often a very important reason to save for: a holiday, a deposit on a car or a house, a wedding. The feature of this type of saving is that expenditure can be predicted. Some parents take out life assurance policies shortly after their children are born for a private education or eventual wedding.

For emergencies

These are the events whose dates or even occurrence cannot be predicted. Sickness or a car breakdown cannot be forecast and can be quite unexpected.

Some money put by for this 'rainy day' will be very useful as the alternative, when accidents occur, is to borrow.

For the family

As parents get older, or become grandparents, they begin to think of providing for the younger family members to give them 'a start in life'. This motive could be important, for instance, if house prices continue to rise rapidly, placing homes beyond the financial reach of young borrowers.

For an increase in wealth

Less spending today should mean more wealth and more income in the future. This motive is a deliberate decision by the saver to try to become richer. This is helped where interest rates exceed inflation. Some people are traditionally thrifty. They may continue to save even when inflation is much higher than the interest rate they receive from their savings.

To establish a track record

If people can show that they can save a reasonable sum each month, then lenders will be more disposed to grant credit to them.

For old age

With people living longer and retiring earlier, more of us will need to be saving harder (during a shorter working life) for a longer old age. Moreover, the government is concerned about the cost of state provision for older people, so that we cannot rely on our retirement pensions as the current generation of retirees have done. Personal pensions (including stakeholder pensions), ISAs and rental income from property are three possible means of achieving a reasonable future income.

To fulfil a contract

If you have a life assurance policy or a personal pension, then you have a legal obligation to put the premium or the contribution aside and to pay it to the insurance company or pension fund. These contractual savings can be very important because they are not dependent on the whim of the saver.

The age and responsibilities of a saver will also impact on his or her propensity to save, i.e. the proportion of their income that is invested or saved on a regular basis. This may follow a "life cycle" where different stages of a saver's life generate different needs:

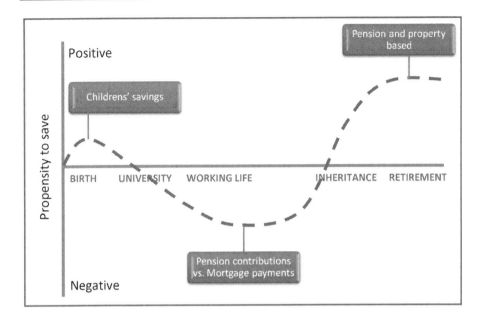

Figure 8.2: The saver's lifecycle

Young people often have savings accounts started for them and may be encouraged to save from pocket money and jobs. As they become students or begin work they have expenditure to meet and may draw on savings for this purpose. During a working life different types of saving become sensible – pensions and life assurance, together with investment in a home (often with the help of a mortgage loan).

Once children "fly the nest", going to university or to work, there may be surplus income that can be saved. In addition, and very sadly, people in their 50s and 60s are the beneficiaries of bequests from their deceased parents. Once a person is retired there may still be surplus income for a while although the focus tends to turn to investments that combine good returns with an acceptable level of risk.

Closely associated with this "lifecycle" is the propensity to borrow. This is legally barred for the under 18s but soon emerges after that with student loans, student overdraft deals, mortgage loans, personal loans and credit cards. In retirement there should be a limited need to borrow, although emergencies and timing differences may still arise. One possibility after retirement, however, is the growing availability of deals whereby individuals can mortgage their home in order to realise a lump sum that can be invested for income generation. This type of facility should suit individuals with valuable homes but little income.

Types of loan account

Loans are rather simpler to categorise. The motivations of personal borrowers are essentially twofold:

1. The purchase of an asset
2. The anticipation of income (liquidity needs)

Asset purchase cannot always be financed from current income or cash-flow, however, a loan repayment may well be within an individual's scope or a business' ability to fund from monthly income or profits. Repayment from various sources is further discussed in Chapter 12.

For a business there may be a need to finance assets before any income can be generated. Straightforward loans are not the only way of doing this but it is a method that many businesses request. For an individual house mortgage and personal loans are popular.

Figure 8.3: Types of loan accounts

Mortgage Loan	*Typically for house purchase and secured on the asset purchased. Loans run for 25 years or longer.*
Personal Loan	*For asset purchases (e.g. car) these have a fixed monthly repayment.*
Credit Card/Revolving Credit	*These set a credit limit and demand a minimum monthly payment. Once repaid the credit can be re-drawn.*
Overdraft	*Set credit limit on a current account. Normally reviewed annually.*

Business loans have similar characteristics to personal finance vehicles but sometimes the terminology is different. A repayment loan, where interest is added monthly, and a regular repayment agreed look the same as a mortgage loan, especially where it is secured on a property. Typically, however, it is called a medium-term loan.

Much personal borrowing is via overdraft or credit card and in most cases the second motivation explains why people request credit from a bank. Individuals will often have expenses such as rent, living costs and travel to fund before they receive their monthly salary or weekly wage. Consider a student starting his or her first job. The salary is paid at the end of the month (in arrears) but the petrol station/sandwich bar/landlord will nearly always want to be paid on delivery or in advance.

Businesses, too, use overdraft facilities since they need to finance the purchase of stock, payment of wages and so on before income is generated. Whilst it is difficult for personal customers to obtain credit from a supplier (such as a grocery store) a business often seeks credit facilities from suppliers. It is essential, therefore, for a bank to know just how much the business is borrowing at any one time. This is discussed further in Chapter 12.

Peoples' expectations of lifestyle and societal norms also create a demand for material things. Note here that people do not have a demand for credit; it is simply the necessary adjunct to their demand for cars, holidays and houses. The alternative would be to make savings from current income and wait.

House mortgages

One of the most common examples of asset purchase via a loan is house mortgage purchase. This is popular in the UK and USA due to a positive attitude towards owning property. This attitude is not shared in all countries in Europe, where property rental is the norm – a factor that the monetary authorities also have to take into account.

In addition to interest rates two key parameters are important in comparing house mortgage products both between different providers and between different countries. These parameters are **loan to value ratio (LTV)** and the maximum loan allowed based on an applicant's income.

The UK mortgage market, in the period leading up to the credit crunch, was fuelled by cheap funding and the propensity to securitise mortgages. This meant that banks could access cheap funds on the inter-bank market and lend them out profitably, often selling the debt obligation to an investor, once the loan was established, and lending the new funds to the next applicant. This fuelled higher house prices (demand outstripping supply) and caused banks to increase the LTV and income multiples to capture more and more borrowers.

Post credit crunch many of the lessons of this profligacy have been learnt as shown in the brief comparison of some countries' approaches to LTV and income in Figure 8.4:

Figure 8.4: Mortgage loans around the world (2013)

COUNTRY	LTV	INCOME MULTIPLE
France	Typically 80% maximum but no statutory limit.	Commercially set but based on total debt and stability of earnings – typically debt servicing is around 33% of eligible revenues.

COUNTRY	LTV	INCOME MULTIPLE
Switzerland	80% maximum set by federal law.	Commercially set – around three times income.
Singapore (tight prudential regulation)	Varies depending on citizenship status, residential status and private or state property.	Determined by total debt servicing requirement (TDSR). Similar to France and based on total debt and prevailing interest rates and incomes but with statutory power.
UK	Commercially set but typically a maximum of 95%* in 2013. LTVs were as high as 120% in the period before the credit crunch.	Commercially set – between 2.5 and six times income.

* 95% is possible for certain buyers via a government guarantee.

In Chapter 12 we explore the canons of lending and, without stealing the thunder of that chapter, it is important to note that the house mortgage problems that fed the credit crunch breached two of the key lending parameters: ability to repay (income multiple) and security (LTV).

Combining deposits and mortgage loans, some banks offer off-set mortgages, allowing borrowers to reduce interest payments based on the level of savings held in linked accounts.

Interest rates

Before we leave the subject of interest-based products and income for banks it is advisable to rehearse the nature of interest rates, themselves. Used by governments and central banks as a key tool to manage national economies they are powerful signals of inflation and expectations.

Nominal interest rates (i) take account of a number of factors:

$$i = r + \pi + l + \sigma$$

Where:

r = real interest rate

π = inflation premium (based on expectations of future price growth)

l = liquidity premium, the premium required for giving up the ability to spend the funds now.

σ = risk premium (i.e. systemic risk of default)

Thus, the interest spread or margin will depend not only on the banker's preferences but also forecasts of future economic conditions.

Having set this formula Figure 8.5 outlines key interest rate types offered by lenders (especially for house mortgages). Consider the funding and risk strategies associated with each of these rate types from the lender's perspective:

Figure 8.5: Interest rate types[15]

RATE TYPE	EXPLANATION
Variable (floating)	Bank standard mortgage rates, constructed based on cost of funds, liquidity and risk premia as above. These may stay static even when base rates change.
Tracker	Based on bank published base rates, central bank rates or the infamous LIBOR . Effective rates are quoted at x% over the base rate. Effective rates change as base rates are amended.
Fixed	Deals can be for periods of two (typical for UK) or five (Germany) or even ten years (Switzerland). Rates are fixed at the start of the agreed period resulting in a fixed repayment amount regardless of movements in base rates.

Non-interest-based products

We saw in Chapter 3 that retail bank profitability is dependent not only on funding and lending, operational costs and bad debts but also on the ability to enjoy "economies of scope", by selling financial products on a fee or commission basis. Fees and commissions are charged for loans too (booking fees for fixed rate mortgages, for example) but the other opportunities fall into the following categories:

 ▶ **Insurance and investment products** – these can emanate from the lending relationship and are fairly generic across sectors and territories.
 ▶ **Payment services** – these also emanate from the basic account relationship but take on different structures depending on territory, technology and sector. We explore this in Chapter 10.
 ▶ **International trade services** – these specialist services are aimed at the financial and physical risks involved in international trade. Even the smallest business can have import and export issues.

---

15 LIBOR is the London InterBank Offered Rate. The average of daily rates offered between banks on the inter-bank market. It was the subject of scandal when it was shown that dealers in banks had colluded to fix the rate at an artificial level. (see Chapter 2).

▶ **Risk management services** – these cover financial risks generally such as interest rate or exchange rate fluctuation.

The last two are outside the scope of this text but are included here for completeness.

To put the importance of non-interest income into perspective, Figure 8.6 lists the ratios of net interest income and other operating income for eight large banks (Scandinavian and EU) based on their 2012 accounts:

Figure 8.6: Ratios of net interest income to non-interest income

BANK	RATIO:1	BANK	RATIO:1
Nordea	1.3	HSBC	1.14
Danske	2.44	Credit Agricole	2.96
DnB ASA	1.96	BNP Paribas	1.17
Skandinaviska Enskilda	0.83	Banco Santander	1.99

Derived from Bankscope (2013)

Retail banks often exist as part of a universal Bank (see Figure 2.2 in Chapter 2) and offer investments, insurance and pensions on behalf of a bank owned (tied) provider. Where retail banks do not have this advantage they can act as brokers offering advice and arranging policies with outside providers.

Insurance products

In a risky world individuals and businesses need insurance to cover financial loss should certain events occur. The business of insurance is, of itself, an extreme form of financial intermediation. Instead of there being deficit and surplus units (borrowers and lenders) there is a whole population of insured entities and a smaller population for whom the risk of loss will become real. One key bit of terminology is that this incorporates insurance and assurance. Insured events may happen – I may become ill. Assured events will happen – I will die (eventually).

There are a number of risks that are insurable but from the perspective of an insurance company/bank these must have certain features:

▶ **Measurable risks** – actual loss that can be quantified in financial terms.

▶ **Chance** – there must be a randomness about the risk. Insurance companies will estimate likely risks for different age groups (car or life risks) or different locations (flood or theft risks).

▶ **Commonality** – there must be a sufficiently large pool of people or companies sharing the same type of risk. However, actual loss should be independent – the randomness factor.

▷ **Insurable interest** – only those who will suffer loss from a particular risk are able to insure against it. It is unthinkable for unconnected parties to insure others' lives. What if, as an "investment", I insured the lives of people boarding a particular ferry in the Mediterranean?

▷ **Public policy** – Where society considers an event to be a crime it is against public policy for insurance to be valid. In 1892, in the UK, Mrs Cleaver was prevented from collecting insurance proceeds following the death of her husband – after all, she had killed him! (*Cleaver v Mutual Reserve Fund Life Association* (1892)1 QB 147)

Figure 8.7 separates key insurable risks into four key types associated with typical bank customers.

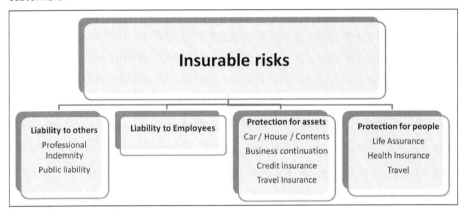

Figure 8.7: Insurable risks

Many of the insurable risks and the policies that can be written to cover them are linked to lending and lifestyle factors well known to a retail banker. For example, the family taking out a house mortgage would want life assurance to cover the adults providing the repayments. In the case of death the loan is repaid. The alternative could be that the bank would have to evict the surviving partner and children following the tragic death of the "breadwinner". We noted reputational risk in Chapter 5 – and here's a profitable way for a bank to avoid it!

Life assurance policies as security are revisited in Chapter 12.

Finally, in this section we note mis-selling scandals that have damaged trust in financial firms and have caused compensation to be paid (see Chapter 2). Payment protection insurance (PPI) and identity theft Insurance are two such scandals related closely to retail banking. Retail banks will do well, in the future, to ensure that appropriate products are sold to appropriate customers.

Investment products

Investments can be undertaken with the help of a professional intermediary who might be a banker but alternatively could be an accountant, solicitor or broker. The investment markets available will depend upon the amount and level of funds available and the risk appetite of the individual or business management team. A range of investment products and markets can be accessed, such as bonds (corporate or government backed), derivatives or equities. In the UK, investment advice is subject to the **retail distribution review (RDR)** and specific payment for the provision of advice is separate from the commission earned on the products themselves.

Under RDR retail banks, amongst other providers, must make it very clear what investment advice will cost or declare that they do not provide advice but simply sell investment products.

Perhaps the most common investment vehicles for individuals and small businesses are pensions. Similar to concept of insurance, the pension fund collects regular contributions during a working life and offers either a *"defined benefit"* – a certain income in retirement or (more rarely nowadays) a pension based on the final salary of the employee. Pension and insurance funds are invested by professional managers in a variety of vehicles including portfolios of shares, government bonds, corporate bonds, property and even works of art.

Pensions are usually considered to be a complex area, and clearly you need to be appropriately authorised in order to advise in this area. This book does not seek to turn you into pensions experts but to reflect on the subject as a clear business opportunity for most banks dealing with customers. This opportunity straddles both the advisory and delivery side.

What gives retail bankers some affinity with investment is the concept of risk. Lenders (see Chapters 11 and 12) consider particular risks that will affect a borrower's ability to repay a loan. Banks as businesses and their regulators consider a wider spectrum of risks that could affect banking business (see Chapter 5).

Investment via a retail bank falls squarely in the range of normal returns for normal risks. Whilst different investors will have different appetites for risk, depending on many factors including age, stage of life or career, tax regimes etc. Figure 8.8 illustrates the range of risks apparent in the financial environment and indicates the potential returns available. The higher the risk the higher the required return – but the higher the chance of capital loss too.

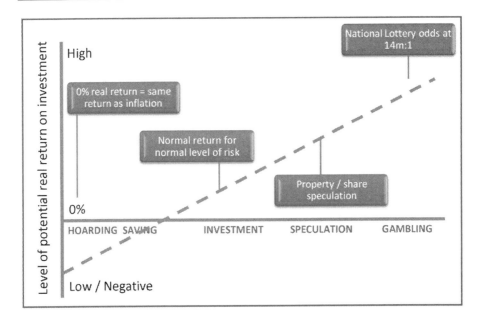

Figure 8.8: Investment risks and returns

International trade products

In order to give a complete overview of the products in the retail banker's catalogue the final two categories of product are included. These are typically for businesses trading as importers or exporters. Key services include transmission of payments, documents and financing of trade.

Bills of exchange have a long history but conceptually are very simple. They are evidence of a debt owed by a buyer to a seller (everyday **cheques** are bills of exchange – albeit drawn on a banker, hence the address of the bank at the top). Typically, bills of exchange are drawn for a term and are "accepted" by the debtor – the person who owes the money. So, once a buyer 'accepts' a bill, it is possible to gain an advance against the bill (provided that the acceptor is creditworthy) much as with factoring and invoice discounting. Bills can be used in 'open account' trading – where the buyer is trusted to pay without further risk management intervention. They can also be used in documentary collections.

Letters of credit are reserved for larger transactions where greater reassurance is required that a bill will be paid when due. In this more complex type of transaction the importer's bank (or a local bank known to the exporter's bank) is involved together with the exporter's bank. Documentation relating to title to the goods traded is sent via the banking system and released only against either acceptance of the accompanying bill or payment.

There is a hierarchy of payment terms – from straightforward invoicing of the importer (trusted buyer) through bill of exchange acceptance by the buyer's bank to **documentary letters of credit**. The fees and charges relating to each will escalate to reflect just how deeply the banking system is involved.

One last observation in this area is that banks can be involved in the international trade process by simply handling documentation through to financing the transactions themselves and/or reducing risk through exchange rate management. The involvement of the bank will be determined by the risks apparent in the specific situation or case.

Basic risk management products

Rather than launch into a description of complex derivative instruments, this text will limit discussion to exchange rate risk in order to illustrate the principles of intermediation embraced by the banker. Those wishing to study this area further are directed to the further reading section at the end of this chapter.

We take the example of an exporter. The export contract to Germany is worth £20,000 GBP. The exporter could avoid exchange risk by asking for payment in GBP (exchange risk is transferred to the buyer). However, in a competitive environment, the exporter has invoiced the buyer in euros – €23,600 (current exchange rate 1.18) and has granted 60 days credit.

The key risk is immediately apparent – that in 60 days, when the payment is due, the GBP/EUR exchange rate may have changed due to interest rate changes, macro-economic events or simple demand and supply of currency. The exporter could receive more than £20,000 for the €23,600 or could receive considerably less. Services offered are summarised in Figure 8.9:

Figure 8.9: Basic foreign exchange products

PRODUCT	BANK SERVICE	EXCHANGE RATE	EXPORTER RECEIVES*
Account	Bank provides a currency account denominated in euros. This is applicable when the exporter has known or expected expenditure in euros in the future.	n/a	€23,600

PRODUCT	BANK SERVICE	EXCHANGE RATE	EXPORTER RECEIVES*
Spot	Bank buys euros at rate prevailing on the day of receipt.	?	?
Forward	Bank agrees to buy euros at a fixed rate normally based on spot rates plus interest.	1.3	£18,154
Option	Bank sells exporter the RIGHT but not the OBLIGATION to sell euros at a fixed rate. If the spot exchange rate is more favourable on the day of receipt the exporter will not exercise the option.	1.3 or lower	£18,154 or more

*   *less bank charges and commissions*

Summary

This chapter has covered:
- Different types of bank savings account
- Different types of loan account
- Interest rates
- Non-interest-based products
- Insurance and investment products and services
- International trade and risk management support

Further reading

Association of British Insurers, 2013, UK Insurance Key Facts 2013, available at https://www.abi.org.uk/

BBC News, 2003, Derivatives – a simple guide, available at: http://news.bbc.co.uk/1/hi/business/2190776.stm

CHAPTER 9

Retail Banking Channels

Objectives

After studying this chapter you should be able to:
- ▷ Describe the features of key retail banking channels
- ▷ Analyse different bank delivery systems
- ▷ Explain how different delivery systems work
- ▷ Outline the practical issues relating to common banking channels
- ▷ Describe the changing trends in delivery systems

Introduction

Modern retail banking has many key drivers. As we saw in Chapter 1 the environment within which retail banks have developed over the past 30 years has been dominated by two major forces: regulation and technology.

Combine these two drivers with the individual banks' objective of optimising rewards for shareholders (making profits) and the focus comes to rest on the much overshadowed area of banking operations.

Regulation under Basel 2 (see Chapter 5) widened the scope of banking risks that had to be backed with available capital to include operational risks. Banks have developed sophisticated monitoring and measurement tools to be able to estimate the risk that, for example, payments systems fail, the bank website goes down or, more traditionally, that a bank branch is subject to flooding or a bank raid. Much is invested in shadow and mirror websites, security and business continuation planning in order to mitigate these risks. This chapter outlines the features and the key risks of bank delivery systems (channels) and goes on to describe how different channels operate together in a portfolio.

Finally, the chapter borrows heavily from the work of my colleague David T Llewellyn in painting a picture of a "virtual" or "contract" bank in the twenty-first-century where the legacy of traditional monolithic retail banks is exchanged for networked outsourcing and shared services made possible by technology and made essential by the drive for cost efficiency.

Legacy systems

Although technology has developed at a rapid pace and start-up banks can take full advantage of it (so far as budgets allow) many banks formed in the twentieth century and have problems emanating from the legacy of older systems. In the next section we consider bank branches – perhaps the oldest "delivery system" but we must not forget the dawn of computerisation in the 1960s and 70s. Banks invested heavily in computer systems to support operations. Such systems were designed to support traditional branch- and product-based banking and have had to be updated and upgraded at huge expense as new business models and technological advances have emerged.

In the 1940s in the UK bank statements for customers were written by hand or typed directly from ledgers held within the branch. Requesting a statement or even a cheque cashing facility at a location other than the account holding branch was fraught with delay.

By the 1970s, branch ledgers had been replaced by central computer systems that recorded the same basic information. This was partly due to the expansion in customer numbers but also the overall costs and flexibility of branch-based systems.

Legacy systems are seen as a barrier to exit from the industry in Chapter 6 as they only have value if they are used to generate revenues and profits rather than as valuable assets in their own right. By the 1990s the computer systems of the 1970s were obsolete, as was the dynamic between customers and branches on which such systems were based.

Figure 9.1 displays the basic mid-twentieth century delivery channel for retail banking product – the bank branch and its relationship with a typical customer. The branch was the conduit for all interactions and as products were added to the bank's portfolio the branch banker became a multi-faceted professional.

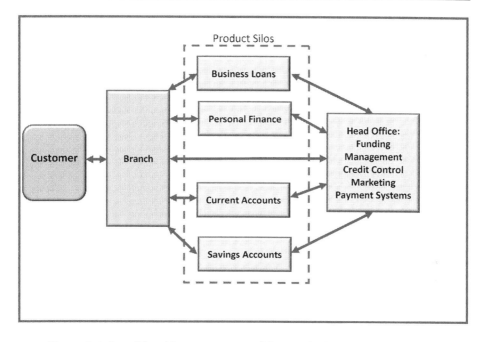

Figure 9.1: Retail banking systems – mid-twentieth century

The diagram in Figure 9.1 is simplified (of course) and does not adequately reflect the monolithic design of a retail bank – in which the bank owned and controlled its own stationery printers, chequebook producers, transport fleet, regional and area offices, in-house lawyers, training schools....the list goes on.

The key point here is that the branch was the sole interface between the bank and most of its customers and to cater for most business and credit decisions. It was managed by a senior staff member with a salary and remuneration package commensurate with his or her professional status and responsibility. An excellent series of pictures published on The Telegraph website (Telegraph, 2013) illustrates the grandeur and professionalism of this era in a way that my words cannot match.

Head offices of banks provided funding, marketing, legal and product design etc. and operated branches much as a franchise similar to McDonalds. The branch manager was the ruler of all (typically) he surveyed, running the branch as an individual business with little "interference" from Head Office.

In the 1980s and 1990s, however, banks began to adopt new technologies and ideas such as telephone banking. The UK's first and most successful telephone bank was First Direct (part of HSBC). The secret "Project Raincloud" was launched in 1989 and grew swiftly. It reached 100,000 customer accounts by 1991 and 250,000 by 1993. Other banks hesitated in their response to this success.

Behind the scenes, however, First Direct had been designed as an enormous branch, using Midland Bank (later HSBC) branches to garner deposits, ATMs and Midland's access to cheque and credit clearing and sophisticated telephone systems (call centres) to interface with customers 24 hours a day, 7 days a week.

By 1992, however, banks had begun to transform into their twenty-first century selves as the narrative around branches and systems design in this chapter goes on to illustrate.

Delivery systems

The different delivery systems available for bank products and interactions are described here in their roughly chronological order of appearance. Chapter 10 focuses on payments systems in particular and it can be seen that the development of payments has a large impact on channel development.

This section focuses on the design, functions and purpose of different channels or delivery systems. Each system has its own costs of establishment and maintenance which must be amortised over its useful life but also different transaction costs. Different physical and security risks are also apparent.

Bank branches and the transport used to service them were a clear target for armed robbery from the days of Jesse James to the Great Train Robbery and the Brinks Mat robbery. In the twenty-first century these risks are much reduced but the focus has turned to cyber-crime, identity theft and plastic card fraud.

One similarity exists, however, between cash and e-money theft – it is the bank that has to pay for the losses and so much effort is expended in reducing and even avoiding the risks.

Branches

Bank branches around the world (and all full-service retail banks must have them) share a design that recognises historic roots and legacy systems but also reflects the demands of the modern consumer. The functions of a branch have changed considerably from being the sole point of contact between customers and the bank to being one of a number of interlocking and parallel mechanisms.

Bank branch numbers around the world are illustrated in Figure 9.2. This shows selected territories and the number of commercial bank branches per 100,000 adults. Although Brazil is showing high numbers and high growth at a current 46.2 branches per 100,000 adults it is outstripped by Bulgaria at 58, Luxembourg at 88 and Spain at 89.

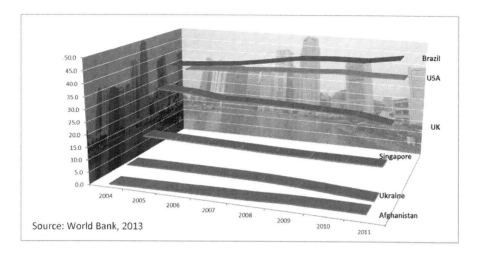

Source: World Bank, 2013

Figure 9.2: Bank branches per 100.000 adults

In the UK a typical bank branch of the mid-twentieth century reserved about 20% of its floor-space for customers. The remaining 80% was to accommodate processing systems for payments, securities and lending clerks, storage space for old cheques and records and staff rest areas. Also, the location of the branch was likely to be in a town square or on a high street. Figure 9.3 shows a schematic diagram of a traditional mid-twentieth century branch.

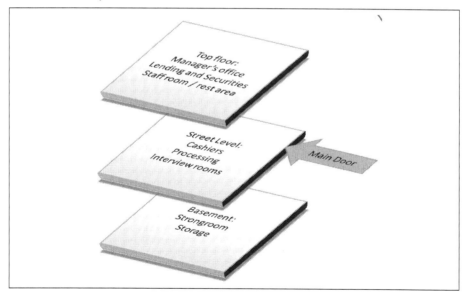

Figure 9.3: Bank branch layout – mid twentieth century

By the late 1980s the paradigm shift from a product-based to a customer and customer data-based busind ess model for banks was beginning to develop. Processing capacity for payments, personal and mortgage loans, ansecurities was moved to regional or national centres. Midland Bank's pioneering "outsourcing" of paper cheque and credit processing from branches in 1989 – 1991 to District Service Centres (later sold by the bank to an independent operator) was echoed by other institutions as the transformation of bank branches began.

Today, typical bank branches are far more "customer-oriented" and almost reverse the staff/customer floor-space ratio so that 80% of floor space is available to customers in open plan settings for ATM transactions, interviews, and formal and informal interactions with staff.

Apart from cashier positions, bank staff no longer hide behind bandit screens. Staff training is typically "on the job" and sales-oriented rather than processing-oriented. With corporate business transacted via separate offices, securities work outsourced or centralised and much personal and small business lending automated there is no need for highly experienced, widely trained branch managers. Branches can be run far more as sales outlets of a central Head Office, rather than franchises with business models of their own.

Figure 9.4 updates Figure 9.3 to today. Branch functions reflect the advances in technology and the strategic move towards more cost-efficient processing of standardised products for a mass market.

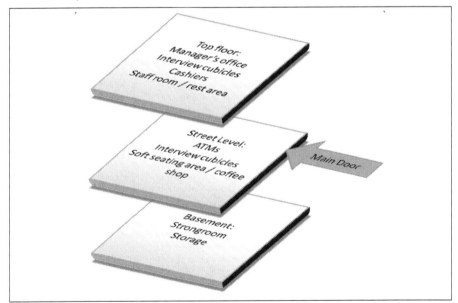

Figure 9.4: Bank branch layout – today

In addition, the bank branch of today is far more likely to be positioned in a shopping mall, on an industrial estate or city centre – with a commensurate reduction in numbers of branches serving remote communities.

The UK example is given as one series of developments. Other states, with different regulations (USA) still retain large numbers of small branches to support a banking landscape with fragmented federal and state regulation. Singapore, however, as an example of an advanced economy with a high percentage of the population "banked" has a relatively small numbers of bank branches per head of population. This is due to a combination of technology, the market (in which there are only a small number of large banks) and geography – Singapore is a tiny country and proximity to a bank branch is not an issue.

ATMs

Automated Teller Machines (ATMs) have been in existence since the early 1960s and have advanced as technologies for plastic cards and telecommunications have developed over the decades. The modern ATM carries out a number of functions (although many banks use separate machines for different functions partly to avoid queuing problems):

- Cash withdrawals
- Cheque and cash deposits
- Balance checking
- Bank statement printing or requests
- Mobile phone top-ups
- Transfers between predetermined accounts
- Loading credit onto stored value cards

As with bank branches the international picture is varied. World Bank data from 2009 is summarised in Figure 9.5:

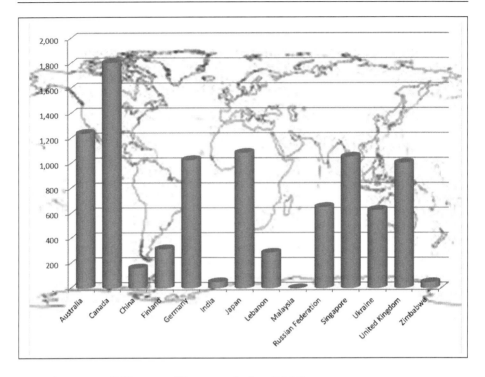

Figure 9.5: ATMs per million population (2009)

ATM operators normally ensure that ATMs are sited in well-lit places and carry warnings to legitimate customers not to allow their transaction to be overlooked. Twenty years ago all ATMs were outdoors but with retail branch re-design some have migrated indoors where transactions can be safer.

ATMs are no longer the sole preserve of banks. Cash handling companies quickly saw the value of installing their own ATMs at non-bank locations (Supermarkets, airports, motorway service areas). The business model was simple: non-bank ATMs charge a fee for the use of the ATM. For independent operators this is the main source of revenue. For some banks this covers the cost of data transmission to the cardholder's bank and, of course, the lost interest on money held as cash.

Figure 9.6 illustrates the relatively straightforward ATM system and pertains whether the ATM is situated at a bank branch or offsite or is operated by an independent company. The ubiquity of card schemes (Visa and MasterCard – see Chapter 10) has also allowed co-operation between banks in ATM reciprocity. In this way customers of one bank can access limited services via the ATM of another bank (even internationally). Fees can be waived in domestic markets but do apply for international transactions.

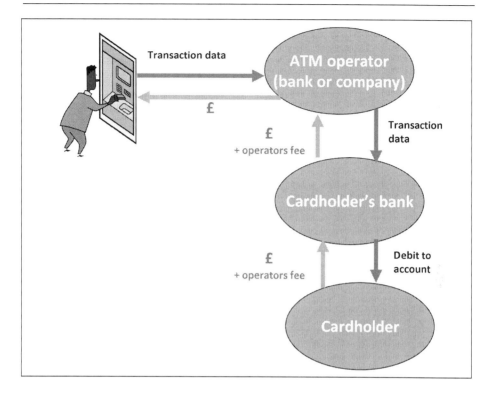

Figure 9.6: Anatomy of an ATM transaction

Key sources of loss in ATM transactions relate to "copying" of ATM card details through the use of sophisticated scanners and cameras that criminals attach to bank ATMs. Although the customer is asked to be vigilant these devices are often miniaturised and well concealed. Once card data is read the criminals can buy goods or withdraw cash until the cardholder realises that there is a problem and reports it to the bank.

Queuing problems at ATMs (and in retailers) are also cited as opportunities for thieves. Cardholders need to shield their PIN from passers-by. Once the PIN is obtained the card can be stolen by a pickpocket and used until reported lost.

Phone banking

At one level **phone banking** simply replaces the bank branch with a 24-hour, 7 day a week call handling centre. The early pioneer of this in the UK was First Direct (see above) in 1989 although the basic idea really originated in mail-order catalogue business in the USA.

One crucial difference between face-to-face branch banking and telephone banking (and its modern equivalents) is the need to identify the caller. As noted in Chapter 7 the advances that made direct banking possible could not overcome one of the basic bank duties to its customers – confidentiality. Phone banking meets this issue in three ways:

- ▶ **Passwords**: memorable words; memorable dates; answers to predetermined questions such as "what was the name of your first pet?" are established at the outset of the relationship.
- ▶ Phone banking **contracts** are agreed with customers so that the customer shares responsibility for keeping the security codes and passwords undisclosed.
- ▶ Because they may be overheard callers are asked only for certain letters from their memorable words or passwords.

Phone banking uses what are termed "inbound call centres" either operated by a bank directly or outsourced. Inbound centres offer product support, enquiries and more sophisticated loan applications. Banks also use "outward call centres" but these are a sales mechanism rather than a delivery channel.

Early call centres in the UK were UK-based, staffed by trained employees and were able to offer a "triage" service whereby the caller could be swiftly identified and then diverted to a supervisor or different functional area depending on the nature of the enquiry. First Direct still operate in this way with call centres in Leeds and in Scotland. Its parent company HSBC, however, uses its own centres located in different parts of the world with a "triage" system that diverts calls to other centres depending on the issue. For UK-based HSBC customers phone calls are routed to HSBC Malta where HSBC have found a good supply of well-educated, English speaking staff and overall costs lower than the UK.

Different banks operate via independent call centres in the UK or in India, South East Asia or Eastern Europe. These centres must balance costs against customer satisfaction but can offer specialisation, economies of scale and synergies for banks and customers alike.

One interesting facet of the call centre that has caused banks, in particular, to withdraw from overseas providers to the UK, is the accent of the operator. North Eastern UK accents (Newcastle/Northumbria), Scottish and Irish accents are favoured, giving rise to the clustering of call centres in these regions. Other cultural factors are also important in the choice of location resulting in a migration away from India, for example, to Europe for EU-based banks.

Internet

The advent of the **internet** and in particular the cumulative effect of additional functionality and interactivity, typically described as Web 2.0 almost completes the shift of processing capacity from bank staff to customers.

Figure 9.7 illustrates clear phases of internet development embraced by banks:

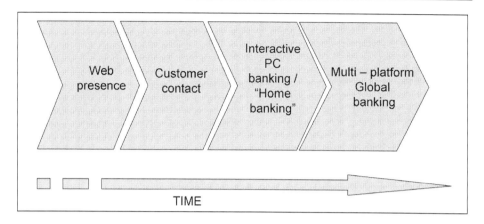

Figure 9.7: Evolution of internet banking

The first breakthrough came in the 1990s with "**Home Banking**", providing consumers and businesses that had telephone linked personal computers to access and interact with bank records to enable balance checking, inter-account transfers and facilitated predetermined bill payments. This has evolved into a functionality that embraces internet and mobile phone interaction, loan application and pretty much all of the tasks previously performed by bank staff in traditional branches or via phone banking.

We noted in Chapter 6 on banking competition that this technology allowed *de-novo* banks to enter the market free of the burden of legacy systems. In a free market economy it can be seen that such competition enhances development.

Mobile phone banking

As with the internet this channel has developed alongside the relevant technology. Clearly, voice calls can be seen as a sub-set of phone banking/direct banking. The expansion of SMS messaging allowed for balance and credit limit alerts to be offered. Notification that an item, if paid, would exceed an agreed credit limit gives the customer an opportunity to transfer funds from elsewhere to meet the item and to avoid charges for an unauthorised overdraft.

There's more on mobile phone payment systems in Chapter 10 but they are included here to illustrate the expansion of internet based-banking into **Smartphone Application** functionality. Mobile phone apps allow smartphone users to perform a variety of tasks that can also be executed on line, via the internet or by phone. Although banks use this channel non-bank competitors such as companies offering short-term consumer ("payday") loans have been swift to adopt it both for advertising and for loan applications.

The inclusion of mobile phones as a separate delivery channel also looks into the future and the opportunities for banks and non-banks to compete and to offer services in areas that are served well by mobile phone networks but not by banking networks (sub-Saharan Africa, rural communities, developing nations).

The balanced channel portfolio

We have now come to a point where various chapters come together. Consider the variety of banker/customer interactions described in Chapter 7 and the list of bank products and services described in Chapter 8. We also acknowledge the systems supporting payment transactions (Chapter 10) and those deployed to grant credit, especially to consumers (Chapter 11).

Whilst different banking channels have similar but different functionality it is clear that many full-service retail banks offer a complete range of channels in order to respond to the different preferences of their customers.

Figure 9.8 shows the channel preferences of two possible customers – Alfie and Isabelle.

Channel: Interaction	Branch	ATM	Phone	Internet / mobile
Communications	♀		♂	♂
Account servicing	♀			♂
Transactions		♀		♂
Credit products	♀		♂	♂
Other Financial products	♂♀			

Figure 9.8: Channel preferences

Alfie is male, 35-years old and a busy professional. He is confident to transact business via the internet and finds it convenient when on the move or at weekends. However, when Alfie wants to discuss more complex products such as pensions or life assurance he prefers to meet face-to-face in a branch office. Isabelle is female and in her 70s. More traditional in her preferences and lifestyle she enjoys the personal contact at a branch and is not confident on line. Alfie does recall, however, that when he was a 20-year-old student his preference profile looked exactly like Isabelle's.

Getting the channel mix right, therefore, is important for a retail bank. Design will be based not only on costs and efficiencies but also the customer base, age profiles, confidence levels and product complexity parameters.

Twenty-first century banking operations

The twenty-first century bank has clear objectives – to serve the interests of shareholders (mainly in terms of return on equity) within a complex and changing environment. Bank operations can be seen as a necessary cost of being a retail bank but a cost that can be minimised without a significant deterioration in service quality.

The key factor that drives the operational design of the twenty-first century bank, however, is not cost or preferences, or products but recognition of what banking is all about. Chapter 2 outlines the financial intermediation core of a bank. Chapter 3 goes on to describe what is seen on a bank balance sheet. What is not shown, however (as it has no accounting value), is the banking asset of information.

Banks create, hold, analyse and use information on their customers as readily as they hold and use deposits of money. Figure 9.9 contrasts with Figure 9.1 at the start of this chapter.

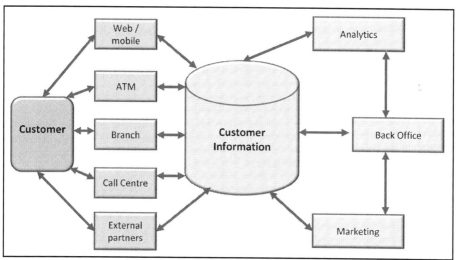

Figure 9.9: Retail banking systems –21st Century

The recognition that customer information, rather than banking products and services, are at the centre of operational design gives rise to a picture of today's retail bank. Branches are simply one of a number of different channels through which customers can access services. Bank retention of data on interactions at a market and at an individual level aids design, facilitates planning and provides flexibility and a chance to move away from legacy systems in a way that does not damage business relationships.

Head Office functions in relation to customer information add an analytical dimension and allow for targeted marketing and pro-active design of existing and new systems.

One final twist for the twenty-first century bank is the recognition that a bank does not have to provide all of the services and functions required to run its business – these can be outsourced or provided via shared service centres. The 1996 work of David T. Llewellyn is summarised in this chapter's final figure. Figure 9.10 shows the various functions of a retail bank described in various parts of this book.

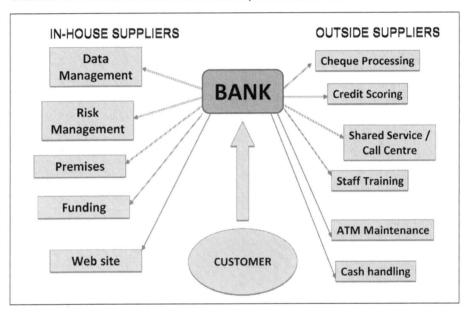

Figure 9.10: The "virtual" bank

As far as the customer is concerned the bank is the same as it has always been but, behind the scenes, key processes and functions are carried out by outside bodies. A number of the outsourced functions relate to routine and frequent operations such as payment transactions and credit scoring (bought in from credit reference agencies). On the diagram it shows that data management, premises management and maintenance of the website are performed in-house but this is not a fixed rule. Any or all of these functions can be outsourced.

What is left for the retail bank is the pure heart of banking – risk management. As we have seen, regulation recognises a number of risk areas for banks. Simply outsourcing supply of functions to providers does not eliminate risk but it can help a bank to manage and minimise it as each party shares risks and takes rewards. It can also introduce new risks such as "agency risk" a corollary to using a third party to deliver bank branded services. But that discussion is for another day and another book.

Summary

This chapter has covered:
- Details of domestic banking channels/delivery systems
- Analysis of different delivery systems
- Practical issues relating to different channels
- Changing trends in delivery systems

Further reading

Croxford H, Abramson F and Jablonowski A, (2005), *The Art of Better Retail Banking – Supportable Predictions on the Future of Retail Banking*, Wiley, Chichester.

Llewellyn D, (1996), *Banking in the 21st Century: The Transformation of an Industry*, Loughborough University Banking Centre.

The Telegraph, (2013), From Top Hats to Metro Bank: a history of British Banking in pictures. [online] available at: http://www.telegraph.co.uk/finance/personalfinance/consumertips/banking/7916201/From-top-hats-to-Metro-Bank-a-history-of-British-banking-in-pictures.html

The World Bank, (2013), Commercial bank branches (per 100,000 adults), [online], available at: http://data.worldbank.org/indicator/FB.CBK.BRCH.P5

CHAPTER 10

Payments and Payment Systems

Objectives

After studying this chapter you should be able to:

▶ Analyse different payment systems
▶ Explain how different payment systems work
▶ Outline the legal issues relating to common payment types
▶ Describe the changing trends in payment systems
▶ Explain the differences between different domestic payment systems

Introduction

In order to be effective intermediaries and to comply with their legal obligations to customers, banks have, over the years, devised and delivered a wide variety of payment methods to enable customer instructions to be followed swiftly and efficiently. Banks have become the custodians of payment systems in many states around the globe since it is in their interest to garner deposits efficiently and to build trust with account holders.

This chapter looks briefly at the nature of payment systems, focusing on the most recent twenty-five years of development as these have seen massive growth in payment numbers and massive innovation in payment methods. The chapter goes on to review the qualities of payment systems, underlining the shift from cash to electronic and plastic card payments in the new millennium.

A theory of payments?

It seems rather grandiose to suggest that there is a theory of payments that can have universal applicability. However, the data from different economies and legal systems can be analysed and reviewed in order to determine key factors affecting the payment systems offered and used by bank customers.

The importance of banks to the global economy and to national and local well-being is supported by the fact that the World Bank regularly surveys and reports on the development of systems. Emerging from this series of surveys is the model outlined in Figure 10.1:

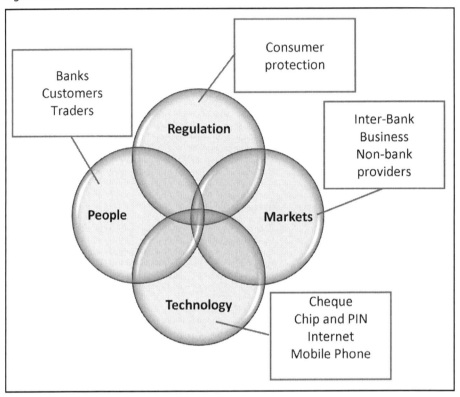

Figure 10.1: The payments environment

Every nation on earth will have a different environment and culture within which payments systems develop. In the UK, for example, the 150 year plus history of cheques is almost at an end. In 2011 The Payments Council, recognising that only 7% of the declining volume of cheques was guaranteed by a card, withdrew the scheme, limiting the acceptability of cheques from consumers. However, there are significant pockets of consumers, charities and businesses still reliant on paper cheques. This caused the banks to remove a threat to withdraw cheques completely.

From World Bank data (2011) Figure 10.2 provides a snapshot of two developed nations' usage of non-cash payments. There are significant differences in usage patterns between Singapore and Canada as explained below:

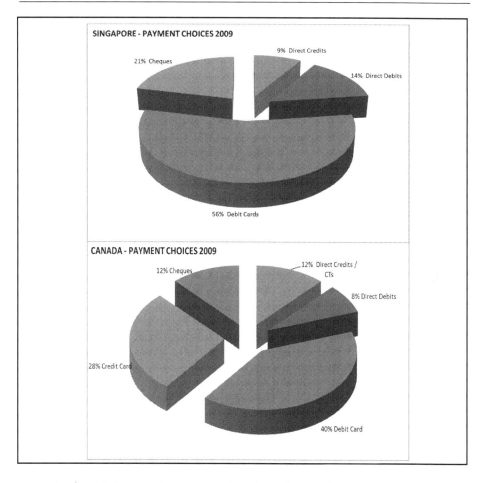

Figure 10.2: Non-cash payments in selected countries

Canada, like the USA is a society reliant on credit with excellent credit reference data on consumers and businesses. Canada also enjoys the latest technologies, mobile phone coverage and broadband internet access. Bank regulation is strong without limiting the efforts of banks to grow their markets. Canada's population of almost 40 million is affluent and its economy well developed. However, Canada is also vast with considerable geographical challenges and a largely conservative population located in a small number of regions.

The Canadian environment gives rise to a large proportion of electronic payments and a large proportion of credit card transactions. Credit cards are widely held and credit information on consumers at a high level. Cheques also retain a significant market share (compared to 3.7% of non-cash transactions in the UK), possibly due to the geographical challenge of the scope of e-banking.

Singapore, by contrast, is geographically tiny. This equatorial paradise has a population of 5.3 million. Bank regulation is very tight and consumer access to credit is limited. Singapore has highly advanced 3G and 4G phone networks and broadband. The reasonably affluent population is well educated and hard working.

Cheques are much in evidence in this conservative society as are debit cards. Credit cards, due to the restrictions on personal credit, are missing from Figure 10.2. In both countries cash is still a significant force. Card charges in Singapore in times of low interest rates can expand cash transactions significantly as consumers consider cash to be "free" to use.

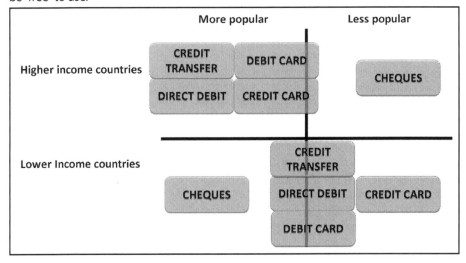

Figure 10.3: Analysis of payment preferences

Analysis of World Bank data is summarised in Figure 10.3 showing that income levels and economic development have a significant influence on the payment choices offered by banks. This, however, fails to explain the considerable importance of mobile phone payments in countries such as India, Kenya and Finland. Here, the key drivers are the availability of technology and the lack of traditional banking infrastructure, especially in poorly populated areas.

The qualities of retail payment systems

Every retail payment system has **three** key parties:
- The customer
- The trader or retailer, and
- The bank

To be acceptable a payment system must provide benefits to each of them. There are a number of ways in which we can review, classify and analyse payment systems. This text uses the **T.E.S.C.O mnemonic**.

The T.E.S.C.O mnemonic outlines five key features of payment systems, each of which need to be viewed from the three perspectives of bank, retailer and customer. This method of analysis and categorisation shows why customers prefer cash but that this preference is not always shared by the other two parties.

In brief, the T.E.S.C.O mnemonic stands for:

▶ **T** – Time (processing time as well as value date)
▶ **E** – Expense (processing and value dating costs)
▶ **S** – Security
▶ **C** – Convenience (including portability and acceptability), and
▶ **O** - Other attributes (such as gold having intrinsic value)

Figure 10.4 uses T.E.S.C.O to analyse cash and illustrates why flexible and convenient cash is still the favourite with consumers. Retailers and banks, however, are motivated to reduce the level of cash transactions in favour of automated payments and debit cards. Plastic cards generate faster and cheaper electronic payment messages when used in conjunction with retailer **point of sale (POS) terminals**. This motivation also underpins the offer of "cash back" from retailers at the point of sale.

Figure 10.4: The Qualities of Cash

CRITERION	EXPLANATION	CUSTOMER	RETAILER	BANK
T – Time	Duration of transaction including value date.	Loss of interest from point of drawing cash – but normally handling small amounts.	Time-consuming at checkout but even more so in collecting, storing, counting and banking cash.	More counting, checking, holding, remitting and redistributing required of banks – huge time delays.
E – Expense	Cost in terms of operational and opportunity costs (interest lost).	Transaction cost if charged at ATM, loss of interest.	Security equipment and transit is costly. Value only when credited to an account.	Cash in tills and ATMs is a necessary asset but an unproductive one. Costs are as for retailers with security and management. ATM reciprocity and outsourcing can reduce this.

CRITERION	EXPLANATION	CUSTOMER	RETAILER	BANK
S – Security	Safety and legal redress.	Theft and forgery are problems but, again, individuals carry small amounts.	Handling large sums of cash is always a security risk.	As for retailers.
C – Convenience	Acceptability, divisibility.	Highly acceptable in many locations and divisible. Not useful in foreign countries.	As for consumers.	As for consumers.
O – Other	Other attributes.	None.	None.	None.

Key domestic payment systems

This section describes the key domestic/consumer payments systems offered by banks. To put each into context Figure 10.5 provides volume and value data for UK payments estimated for 2013, together with average values per transaction. Clearly cash and debit cards are used for relatively small values. We have already noted the demise of cheques in the UK but they do remain popular for relatively large transactions. Direct credits, largely salary payments, boost the average values of this mechanism whilst CHAPS outstrips everything else in terms of values transmitted and the average value of transactions at over £2 million.

Figure 10.5: Payment volumes and values in the UK (2013 est.)

PAYMENT TYPE	VOLUME (M)	VALUE £M	AVERAGE VALUE
Cash	20,104 (48%)	277,447	£13.80
Debit Card	9,033 (21%)	415,695	£46.02
Standing Order	536 (1%)	254,992	£475.74
ATM	3,035 (7%)	207,499	£68.37
Cheque	817 (2%)	824,885	£1,010.12
Credit Card	2,176 (5%)	155,637	£71.53
Online	398 (1%)	175,435	£441.16
CHAPS	37 (0%)	78,606,159	£2,110,799
Direct Debit	3,705 (9%)	1,210,241	£326.62
Direct Credit	2,339 (6%)	3,833,559	£1,638.64

Source: The Payments Council and Keith Pond.

Cash

For retail banks **cash** is a necessary but costly payment mechanism to offer. The T.E.S.C.O analysis in Figure 10.4 shows that for banks the volumes of cash required give rise to security and transaction time issues. With the notable exception of the Eurozone cash is typically not acceptable outside a country's borders. In Chapter 4 we noted the acceptance of US dollar in the Ukraine when the domestic currency was devalued – but this was at a time of crisis. Security and handling costs are the biggest headaches for the retail banks and yet consumers have a large level of demand for cash and do not expect to pay for the privilege of receiving their own cash from an ATM.

Central banks in Australia and Singapore have already issued plastic banknotes to extend durability and lower longer-term costs. The Bank of England is planning to do the same.

Cheques

A **cheque** is defined as an instruction in writing to a banker ordering him to pay a third party the amount stated.

Cheques were a popular method of payment in the nineteenth and twentieth centuries, initially locally but then nationally once transport networks offered secure and swift transmission. In the UK cheque growth can be seen following the expansion of railways in the nineteenth century. In the twentieth century road networks allowed exchange (clearing) of cheques via a central location (initially London) overnight.

As with cash, cheques give rise to cost and security considerations for retail banks. Physical transmission of cheques has been replaced by transmission of a cheque image but the risks of forged or missing signatures, incomplete or unclear written instructions or post-dating of cheques remains.

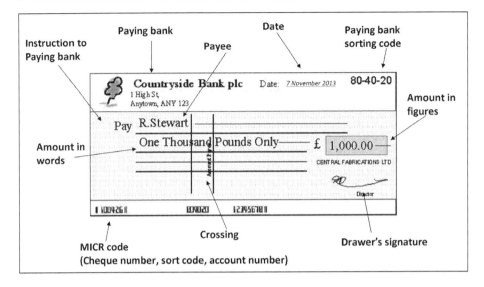

Figure 10.6: Anatomy of a cheque (UK)

Figure 10.6 illustrates the many facets of the cheque in the UK – a cheque format familiar to many parts of the world. US cheques carry all of the same key elements: The payee; the amount in words and figures (the amount in words being definitive); the address of the bank on which it is drawn; and the signature of the customer (drawer).

The process of cheque collection, in part, underpins the retention of bank branches (see Chapter 9). Most UK banks out-sourced this processing function to regional centres in the 1990s and then to private contractors as volumes fell. In the USA cheque clearing (also declining) is undertaken either locally between banks or via the Federal Reserve with paper cheques being physically driven or flown to drawee banks for payment.

Cheques are preferred by business users for reasons of convenience and because cheques allow businesses to enjoy a "float" whilst a cheque is being cleared and before it is applied to a bank account. A cheque also provides evidence of receipt and evidence of non-payment should it be returned unpaid.

Debit cards

Debit cards were introduced in the 1980s and are fast becoming the payment mechanism of choice in face to face, phone and internet based transactions. Debit cards also function as cash cards in ATMs. Depending on the global card scheme adopted by the issuing bank (e.g. MasterCard or Visa) they can also be used in transactions abroad.

A word of caution here, however, as the author well knows; banks do like to be advised when the cardholder is to use the card abroad. Transactions can be blocked if the bank computer systems detect unusual behaviour (larger than normal amounts, different places, increased frequency of use). American Express pioneered "expert systems" to highlight unusual transactions as a method of combatting fraud.

As a method of payment they act as a 'reusable cheque' for any amount. Retailers are electronically linked to banks in order to obtain on-line authorisation for higher level payments, to access details of the latest stolen cards and to send transactions electronically for accounts to be updated. Thus, the debit can reach the customer's account instantaneously. Originally debit cards operated on magnetic strip technology and required verification of most transactions by customer signature. As with cheques fraud became relatively easy and so banks had to devise new systems to prevent losses.

Key parts of a typical debit card are shown in Figure 10.7. The "security digits" on the signature strip on the card are used in phone and internet transactions. The latter are also protected by separate security checks carried out by card issuers.

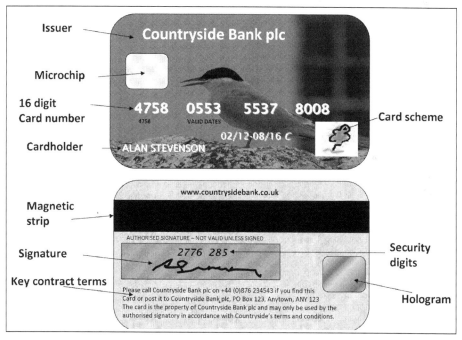

Figure 10.7: Anatomy of a debit card

Chip and PIN technology appears to have halted the steady rise in card fraud but criminals still find ways to bypass the systems adopted and so eternal vigilance is needed by banks. Leading up to the launch of the new technology UK Chip and PIN, banks began issuing new cards to all cardholders. From 14 February 2006 it was expected that most transactions using debit (and credit) cards would be via Chip and PIN. The difference between the technologies lies within the unique microchip embedded in each card. The chip encodes the customer PIN and includes other identifying data that are difficult to replicate. Because of this the customer must only use a PIN rather than a signature to verify transactions.

Full debit cards can be linked to an overdraft or credit facility granted by a retail bank. For accounts that are required to run in credit, however, *MasterCard*, through its European subsidiary *Maestro*, offers the *Solo* card – *Visa* offers *VisaElectron*.

Credit cards

Credit cards were introduced in the USA in the 1940s and were issued for specific purposes (fuel purchase, airline tickets etc.). In the 1950s the charge card *Diner's Club* was unveiled. This granted no credit to the holder but pioneered (with *American Express*) the technology and clearing arrangements between retailers, banks and cardholders.

The breakthrough for modern credit cards came in 1958 with the launch of *BankAmericard*, the first plastic card backed by a revolving credit facility. This card was franchised and copied around the world and became the foundation of the Visa system. The UK saw its first credit card in 1967 when Barclays launched its *Barclaycard*, using computer systems developed by the Bank of America. In 1972 the *Access* credit card was launched by the Joint Credit Card Company (JCCC) owned by Lloyds, Midland and National Westminster banks. Since then, *Access* cards have been offered by Royal Bank of Scotland and Bank of Ireland.

Access was restrictive in its membership policy, being the sole UK representative of the *MasterCard* network, based in the USA. The division between Barclays, part of *Visa*, and the other big three banks, part of *MasterCard*, has now ended.

From a technical and security perspective credit cards are the same as debit cards. The inclusion of a revolving credit facility distinguishes credit cards and the business model for issuers shows how remunerative they can be. Credit card issuers derive their income from two sources:

a) commission charged to retailers and others such as hotels and insurance brokers, who accept the card in payment of sales (up to 5% of revenue); and

b) interest charged to cardholders who do not repay all their balance within a set number of days of the date shown on their monthly statement. Each merchant – the technical name for a retailer or outlet – and cardholder is given a limit. For instance, merchants may have a limit of £50 per transaction beyond which they cannot accept a card without authorisation by the card issuer. This is normally done on line but can be by phone call. Cardholders have higher limits, e.g. £7,500, which their total balance at any one time must not exceed.

Figure 10.8 illustrates the flow of data and funds in a credit or debit card transaction. It should be noted that the "merchant acquirer" may be the retailer's bank or may be an outside provider (another bank) since this type of service can be independent of the main banking relationship.

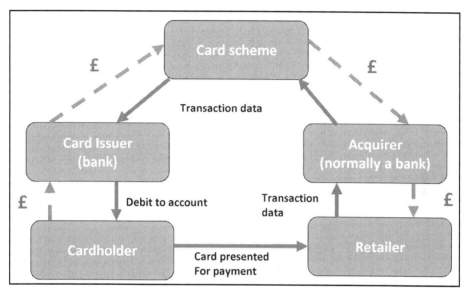

Figure 10.8: Flow of data and funds in a card transaction

With each statement, cardholders are given a wide range of repayment options, from repaying the whole balance to repaying only a minimum payment (equivalent in the UK to interest for the month plus sufficient capital to repay the balance within three years). It is entirely up to the cardholder how much they repay, provided that it is between the maximum and the minimum. This illustrates how flexible a method of payment and repayment a credit card can be. Interest is charged monthly on the outstanding balance, should the amount not be repaid in full. It is calculated from the date of each transaction.

For the vigilant consumer credit cards are convenient and cheap. However, the ease by which credit can be granted, together with the temptation of 0% balance transfer offers by issuers helped to fuel the fragility of the US and UK economies in particular as the credit crunch of 2007 took hold.

The credit crunch has severely reduced the amount of credit card usage and holding of multiple cards as consumers seek to repay debts. Large numbers of consumers, however, have had difficulty in repaying debts so freely acquired and the numbers of insolvencies and repayment programmes has escalated.

Mobile phone payments

A relatively new but growing payment mechanism is via mobile phone. Systems exist to connect a card-reader to a smartphone but this is, strictly, an alternative way of accessing the debit and credit card system. Various business models exist with free card readers and transaction fees at around 2.75% (for example Powa (South Africa/UK) or Square (US)) or paid for card readers (around £100) and lower transaction fees (for example iZettle (Sweden) 1.5% for larger monthly turnover).

Full mobile phone payment systems such as Barclay's *Pingit* in the UK and *MPesa* in Kenya use only mobile phone numbers. The system works by payers registering their mobile phone details with a bank with whom they have a contract for the service. They may also have their bank account with the same bank, although this is not a necessary requirement. The receiver of the funds is contacted by the bank and funds duly remitted.

Figure 10.9 illustrates the transaction flow and the relationships between the different parties.

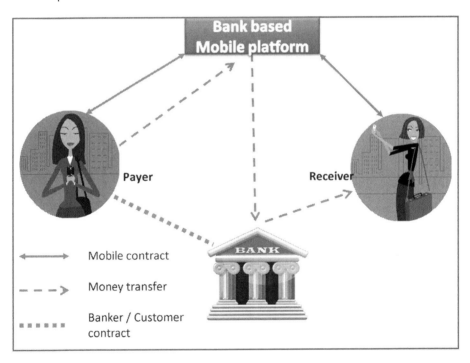

Figure 10.9: Flow of data and funds in a mobile phone transaction

Automated payments

The three key automated payments in use are:
- Standing Orders
- Direct Debits and
- Bank Giro Credits

Standing orders and direct debits, together, are called **pre-authorised payments** as they are set up by the customer in advance and normally for regular payments. The key difference between these two methods is that standing orders are originated by the customer's bank, sending funds to the account of a beneficiary. Direct debits, on the other hand, are originated by the beneficiary by making a "claim" on the bank account of a customer. The customer's bank pays the claim provided it has a clear authority (mandate) from the customer to do so.

With standing orders the bank receiving the order has to take care to establish whether or not the amount to be paid changes from time to time and whether there is a date after which payments cease. Standing orders can be altered only by the customer, in writing. Examples of regular payments where standing orders can be used include annual subscriptions, life assurance premiums, monthly and quarterly rents and mortgage repayments.

Direct debits have several advantages over standing orders:
- The beneficiary is aware of every transaction so that there are no 'unapplied credits' which cannot be traced.
- Most debits are paid by customer's banks with only a small minority being returned for lack of funds.
- If the debit is for a variable amount, and many are, the amount can be increased in line with rising costs.

Safeguards are built into the system to prevent people initiating direct debits which are unauthorised or for excessive amounts. All originators must be approved by their bank and must give an indemnity to reimburse the customer and his or her bank for incorrect debits, e.g. where a computer tape or disc is accidentally processed twice. A further safeguard is that every originator must give adequate notice to customers of a forthcoming change in the amount of a direct debit.

The disadvantages arise mostly with variable amount direct debits. Some customers do not check their statements regularly and so may be unaware of rising subscription rates. If they had to change a standing order they would be alerted to increases and, moreover, might cancel their subscription. This disadvantage from the customers' standpoint is, of course, an advantage to the originating organisations.

Bank credits transferred electronically are a major part of internet and direct banking. Payment details of regular bills are held by the bank and customers trigger these, often adding the amount to be paid via an internet or telephone connection with the bank.

Other domestic payment mechanisms

For the sake of completeness this section simply lists and describes other mechanisms available via banks and building societies:

Bank Drafts	These are cheques drawn on a bank (and, therefore, should not be returned unpaid). Safer than cash they offer a physical payment method for relatively high amounts, e.g car purchase. A fee is charged by the bank for issuing a draft.
Building Society Cheque	Similar to a bank draft but issued by a building society.
CHAPS	The Clearing House Automated Payment System is for large domestic payments that require same-day credit of the beneficiary's account. Transfers to complete house purchases often use a series of CHAPS payments to effect the transaction.

Figure 10.5 shows that in 2013 the average payment via CHAPS was over £2million – nobody wants that to be hanging about in the clearing system overnight!

Competition and co-operation in payments

Lastly in this chapter it is important to recognise that, in many parts of the world, banks not only compete for business using the attractiveness of their payments systems but also co-operate in order that payments between institutions are handled consistently and efficiently.

From Chapters 2 and 3 we note that, strategically and prudentially, it is beneficial for banks to retain money within the banking system, if not within their own bank. Electronic payments between banks achieves that, whilst a cash transaction removes money from banks into people's wallets and pockets or inside the sofa. An apocryphal story suggests that the average car "hides" at least three euros (in coins) in its interior. Good bonuses for car breakers but a loss to the banking system, especially if those cars end up in India or China to be broken up.

Whether payments occur through cheques, plastic cards, mobile payments or internet transfers, therefore, it is important for banks domestically and internationally, to agree common protocols and clearing systems.

Summary

This chapter has covered:
- A brief history of payment mechanisms
- Tools to analyse different payment mechanisms
- Details of domestic payment systems in use today
- A brief outline of the organisation of payments mechanisms by retail banks

Further reading

Payments Council, (2013), [online] available at http://www.paymentscouncil.org.uk/

World Bank, (2011), Payment Systems worldwide – A snapshot - Outcome of the 2010 global payments survey [online]. Available at: https://openknowledge.worldbank.org/handle/10986/12813

CHAPTER 11

Credit Appraisal

Objectives

After studying this chapter you should be able to:

- ▶ Discuss the lending lifecycle
- ▶ State the elements of good credit assessment
- ▶ Explain how lending principles can be applied to different cases
- ▶ Explain the role of credit scoring in personal lending
- ▶ Apply basic lending principles to different cases

Introduction

Whole banking careers have been spent in lending and in taking security for loans and overdrafts, so what can be included in a single chapter can only be very rudimentary. Lending is *the* banking skill and banks can fail if their loans are not repaid, as we saw in Chapter 3. Moreover, banks can forego profits if they do not seize opportunities for good lending, so the subject is very important.

Lending encompasses not only the initial decision to lend (the main part of this chapter) but also the monitoring of the loan or overdraft during its lifetime and the eventual repayment of the loan. The next chapter considers typical securities for bank lending.

This chapter approaches the subject of the initial lending decision by looking at the lending acronym **CAMPARI and ICE**, which recalls important principles of lending, then describes the modern technique of credit scoring. The emphasis in this text is on lending to the personal customer and to the small business. The typical lending products outlined in Chapter 8 are largely for personal customers and the likelihood is that the initial decision to lend will rely heavily on credit scoring rather than judgemental lending techniques. For business lending, however, where businesses are very different and each lending proposition unique, good old-fashioned lending expertise is often used (backed up, of course, by supporting computer analysis of the business's projections or historic accounts).

Linked to this chapter is a case study in small business lending which is presented with a commentary based on the CAMPARI and ICE formula (see Appendix).

Anecdotes about shrewd lenders in the past abound. One branch manager I knew would never lend to anybody wearing sunglasses!! He was either very biased or based his judgement on what this might say about a person's character. Unluckily for that manager the one and only time that he was confronted by an armed robber, that robber was wearing sunglasses!

The lending lifecycle

Unlike most products sold by manufacturers and retailers the credit facility has a lifecycle which means that banks are unable to determine the profitability of an individual loan until it has been fully repaid. Although there are accounting methods used to estimate annual profits the credit crunch has shown that these can be wiped out by subsequent losses on loan assets previously thought to be safe and secure.

For the retail banker the loan lifecycle has a number of inter-linked and inter-woven stages

- Courtship
- Birth
- Life
- Rebirth/renewal
- Death

Much marketing and credit appraisal effort is expended in the *courtship* stage where managers seek new customers or to provide new products to existing customers. *Birth* occurs when a loan, overdraft or other credit facility is granted. This chapter gives an overview of this process.

A loan then has a *lifespan* which is expected to end in successful repayment, in which case the banker could seek to lend again to the customer. Life could otherwise end with the loan facility being re-negotiated or re-financed over a different term or with a different repayment schedule, perhaps because of difficulties encountered by the customer. Some loans end in *death* – where the customer fails to repay and may even go through a legal mechanism such as court action or insolvency. Often these loans result in the bank not obtaining full repayment. Lessons learned from unpaid loans are fed back to those managers marketing and granting loans at the beginning of the lifecycle.

Because the whole of the loan advance topped up with unrecovered monitoring costs and unpaid interest may be lost to the bank the individual loan may end up making a loss and a charge on bank profits. Provided the bank can make profits on its other loan assets these losses can be borne. Where losses are too great, however, the bank itself could fail.

Principles of lending

The principles or 'canons' of lending are generic and apply to large corporations as well as to small personal borrowers. Credit scoring criteria (which we shall look at later) can draw heavily on these factors too.

Credit assessment or appraisal was often seen in the past as a "dark art" practised only by old and experienced bankers often offering little explanation for their decisions. However, thinking about the factors necessary to avoid the key risks in extending credit can actually bring this "dark art" within the grasp of we mortals.

In terms of transferable and study skills a lender needs to be able to assimilate verbal and written information rapidly, analyse data within a specific market environment, communicate effectively with clients and superiors and reach sound, evidence-based, negotiated conclusions. This seems a very tall order but as we shall see this area draws on a number of other disciplines, making it complex, uncertain but highly rewarding.

We saw in Chapters 5 and 6 that the FSA recognises certain risks associated with credit granting. These are largely the risk of non-payment and subsequent loss but also extend to reputational risk (where it becomes known that a bank is a worse than average lender); market risk (where a bank needs to spread its lending across different industries and markets); legal risk, especially where security is taken as collateral; and interest and liquidity risk, especially for large non-syndicated loans.

The key risks we are concerned with, however are:

▷ **Adverse Selection** – The fact that the most creditworthy customers do not need to borrow and only those without current funds of their own request credit. Adverse selection is also heightened by **information asymmetry** the situation where the borrower has information not possessed by the bank which could change its risk assessment and......

▷ **Moral Hazard** – the risk that a borrower can change the level of risk after the funds have been borrowed, unseen by the lender. An extreme example is where a borrower may wish to start a business and borrows from a bank to do this. Rather than invest in the business, however, the borrower uses the funds to gamble and loses everything – including the ability to repay the loan.

The first of these risks is mitigated (but not completely avoided) by gathering as much information about the borrower and the lending proposition as possible. The second risk can be mitigated by using loan covenants or by taking security.

Common acronyms that recall the canons of lending and act as an aid to memory and information gathering are listed in Figure 11.1:

Figure 11.1: Common lending acronyms

ACRONYM	STANDS FOR...
3C's	Character, Capability, Capital
IPARTS	Integrity, Purpose, Amount, Repayment, Terms and Security
4 C's	adds Connection to the 3 C's
CRIS	Character, Repayment, Incentive, Security
PARSERS	Person, Amount, Repayment, Security, Expediency, Remuneration, Services
CAMPARI	Character, Ability, Means, Purpose, Amount, Repayment, Insurance
CAMPARI and ICE	adds Interest, Charges and Extras

It should be noted that in each of the acronyms the criteria concerning the personality or character of the borrower rank highly whilst identification of the security on offer is only considered after repayment has been reviewed. This is very much as it should be. Bad lending propositions do not get better just because security is available; they should be judged on their merits and then security sought to provide for unforeseen circumstances which may prevent repayment coming from the primary source.

One final word of warning, however: Different propositions have different priorities and so the order of the CAMPARI factors will depend on circumstances. A closed bridging loan where funds are guaranteed to be delivered by a solicitor and which is secured on an existing property will be little concerned with a borrower's character. Extending an overdraft, however, will depend heavily on the customer's past record with the bank and their ability to manage a facility.

The following sections discuss the popular acronym – **CAMPARI and ICE**:

Character

The borrower, who seeks to be lent money entrusted to the bank by its depositors, must be of the utmost integrity – somebody who will keep their word and who can be believed. In an ideal world the lender would seek evidence to support the borrower's claims but often has to rely on the person's word and their own judgement of them.

Much relies on a borrower's track record with the bank or, in the case of new borrowers, on the lender's skill and experience in interviews with borrowers or on the borrower's credit history obtained from a credit reference agency.

Modern credit searches will not only reveal past good and bad behaviour in repaying loans and managing credit card debt but will also reveal the extent of a person's borrowing capacity – how many credit cards and loans they possess. The greater a person's access to further borrowing the higher the sensitivity to interest rate rises or personal circumstances changing.

For business borrowers annual accounts are often a source of detailed information about the historic trends for the business. This text is not intended as a lending text and so considerations relating to company accounts will be left alone. Suffice to say, however, that accounts for small businesses are rarely prepared for the banker – much more likely they seek to reduce tax liabilities and so may hide or defer items that the banker would expect to see. Importantly the bank interviews the directors and managers of a business and must also form a judgement about their characters and abilities.

Often bankers will seek corroboration of key accounting data such as turnover – perhaps via the bank account and stocks, possibly by making a site visit to see the assets for themselves.

Ability

This is vital for business, whether or not loans are involved. The borrower must be, at the very least, proficient, if not an expert at their job or in their profession. Is there any hint of incompetence? If the customer has been with the bank for many years, there should be some clues in the bank's database but, if the request is from somebody unknown to the bank, searching but tactful questions must be asked at the interview and evidence sought by way of testimonials or qualifications.

A baker who has had years of experience in working for a large bakery may wish to start up a small bakery of his own. Whilst their technical credentials may be unquestioned their ability to manage others and to run a business must be reviewed.

Means/Margin

How much of his or her own money is the borrower using and how much belonging to other people, including the bank? These figures will be apparent from the request from the customer and it is important to remember that many borrowers under-estimate the amount that they need to borrow.

A good rule of thumb would be that a bank would not wish to put in more money than the borrower. The bank takes an equal risk on the success of the venture (unless secured) but only receives interest on borrowings rather than a share of profits.

How much money is being put into the project by the borrower and how much by the banks and other lenders? The latter could include an HP company or finance house. Business customers often finance themselves partly by delaying payment for goods and services bought from their suppliers but accepting only cash payments themselves. A review of the current liabilities of a balance sheet will give the banker clues here. Family finance is also a source of further borrowing – all of which must be repaid at some time.

Purpose

The purpose of the borrowing is extremely important. When personal loans were launched in 1958, a loan for a holiday would have been rejected because the loan's purpose was unacceptable (not a necessity but a luxury). Today a twelve-month loan for a holiday will often be agreed. Increasingly banks concern themselves far more with the ability to repay rather than the purpose (especially for personal borrowers).

However there is a more important reason why purpose is important. This concerns commercial lending. The purpose for which the loan is used will affect the finances of the borrowing firm, and the cash flow projections for the next two or three years will vary according to the use to which the money is put. For instance, if a firm buys the freehold of its existing shop we can expect to see no rent payments in the cash flow projections – possibly a dramatic change – but if, instead, the money is used to buy stock then we should see cash soon coming into the business from the sales of that stock (assuming that sales are for cash and not credit).

There are two main purposes why customers require loans or overdrafts:

- ▶ To acquire an asset
- ▶ To anticipate income

In addition the bank would wish to ensure that it was not lending for an illegal or nefarious purpose! The bank has its own reputation to think of too.

Amount

In retailing there is a saying – "The customer is always right". In retail banking this can be a dangerous assumption as borrowers often have a need to borrow but cannot calculate how much is needed. The borrower may ask for less than is needed, in the hope of making the request seem more attractive to the lender or because the cash flow forecasts are wrong. Many honest borrowers underestimate their cash needs. Even where a property is to be purchased have the legal and professional fees been considered? Have the running costs incurred before income can be generated been covered?

The type of lending – loan or overdraft – will also impact on the amount required. An overdraft should "turn over" or go in and out of credit whilst a loan is typically fixed at the outset. This is linked to Repayment in the next section.

Repayment and term

How is the loan to be repaid? There are two main sources:

▶ from income, e.g. the sales of a firm's output or the wages/salary of a personal borrower; or

▶ from the sale of an existing asset, e.g. an existing house, as with a bridging loan; an insurance policy maturing as with a loan for a world cruise for a customer in his/her late 50s or early 60s.

Whatever the repayment source, it must be known before the loan is granted and be agreeable to both lender and borrower. Repayment must not stretch the borrower too far. Has the personal borrower shown an ability to save the amount of the monthly repayment in the recent past? How stable is the employment and the salary? Is overtime or irregular bonus payments included in the income figure quoted?

For a business loan – does the business borrower's cash flow forecast cater adequately for regular repayments and interest? Have all likely costs been estimated and deducted? Are there written quotations for things such as building work? Are there contracts for the sales of goods? A common error is for new businesses to look profitable on paper but forget such things as the owner's drawings or tax liabilities.

Here the lender's knowledge of the market and environment in which the customer operates is important. An experienced lender can tell if income and cost estimates are valid or if common costs have been omitted. An objective review using the not so common "common sense" approach is often called for.

This part of the acronym also looks at the period of borrowing. Personal loans can go to five years and home loans are – in theory – for 25 years. However, many people sell their house long before the 25 years are up and take out a new mortgage for the new house. In fact, the average life of a mortgage is only about eight years.

The term of the borrowing is related to the purpose of the borrowing. Funds borrowed by a company to buy stock should be repaid when the sales proceeds of the stock are received – usually within months – although fresh borrowing will then occur to finance more purchases of stock. An overdraft is the appropriate form of bank finance here. However, a loan to buy the freehold site of a factory could be repaid over eight or ten years.

For personal lending, a loan for an annual holiday ought to be repaid before the next holiday, but a loan for double glazing or a new kitchen could be repaid over five to seven years. Loans for plant, machinery or cars should take into consideration the useful life of the asset purchased as it is likely that another loan will be requested at this time to replace the asset and it would be foolish to have a loan outstanding on an asset that has either been disposed of or is no longer of any value.

Insurance (security)

This point is deliberately put last because the decision whether or not to lend should have been made on the other six points. Obviously, lending covered by security must be more attractive than unsecured lending but the availability of security may influence the lender to agree to a doubtful proposition. The questions which must be asked are:

- Is security offered?
- If not, can some acceptable security be found?
- Is the security offered adequate?
- If not, can more be found?
- What is the nature of the security? (see Chapter 12)
- Who will deposit the security?
- When will the security be deposited?

Again, as a general rule, a banker should not extend a loan until the security documentation is complete or, at least, until the security has been deposited.

Additional Insurance, in the strictest meaning of the word, also needs to be considered under this heading. For companies, insuring the lives of key directors will be a comfort to the bank. For personal borrowers insurance to cover sickness, unemployment or death will also be sought.

...and ICE

This brings us to the income for the bank to be gained from agreeing to the proposition:

Interest

Is the margin over LIBOR or base rate sufficient to compensate for any risk involved for the bank? Typically, risky industries (eg: construction) will be quoted a higher margin over base rate (e.g. base rate + 10%) than lower risk ones (eg: agriculture – base rate + 3% or lower). Similarly larger firms with good credit ratings would exact finer rates than sole proprietors. Lastly, secured loans are likely to be cheaper than unsecured ones because of the lower ultimate risk.

Favourable interest rates are one of the reasons for the increasing trend for very large firms to bypass the banks entirely and borrow directly from the markets (disintermediation – see Chapters 1 and 2).

Personal borrowers will be unlikely to have the luxury of negotiating an interest rate. The rate offered will be the bank's published rate and this will vary depending on the type of borrowing undertaken.

Some typical rates are shown in Figure 11.2:

Figure 11.2: Typical lending rates for retail bank products*[16]

PRODUCT (SEE CHAPTER 8 FOR DESCRIPTIONS)	PUBLISHED RATE (% P.A.)	APR (% P.A.)	COMMENT
Overdraft (up to £5,000)	variable	19.93%	Banks will increase this rate if overdraft facilities are breached. Offered rate depends on account type (Standard or Premier etc).
Credit card, (balance transfer deal for a fixed period can be 0%)	16.9%	16.9%	The rate includes the price charged for flexibility and convenience and to cover the high percentage of defaulters.
Personal loan (£5,000 x 5 years)	9.9%	9.9%+	Sometimes interest is added at the outset of the loan, making the APR much higher than the published rate.
House mortgage loan (repayment loan)	2.95%	3.9%	The rate used is a two-year fixed rate. Loans can also be agreed with variable rates.
Business overdraft	7.5% - 26.5%	varies	Rate depends on risk assessment. The higher rate relates to unauthorised overdrafts.

*correct as at 1 August 2013

Commission and fees

In addition to annual interest, borrowers may also be faced with commission, sometimes termed as an "arrangement fee" to be paid when the loan is drawn down. Occasionally it is added to the principal amount borrowed. The difference between commission (charges) and interest is that interest compensates the bank for the risk undertaken whilst commission compensates for the work involved in granting and monitoring the loan or overdraft facility. For instance, a typical arrangement fee for a £100,000 house mortgage loan would be £500 plus any survey fees, legal costs. The bank could also charge a "booking fee" for a fixed interest rate and penalties for early repayment. To

---

[16] Interest rates for much personal borrowing are covered by the Consumer Credit Act 1974. This Act stipulates that banks must display not only the rates they offer but also the APR or Annual Percentage Rate. This takes into consideration the real annual rate paid since interest can be added at the start of the loan or added monthly or quarterly.

establish an overdraft limit of £1,000 on a current account the typical fee would be £25 - £40.

UK banks were under fire by consumer bodies and the Office of Fair Trading regarding so called "penalty" fees for unauthorised overdrafts during 2007-08. The banks "won" this particular battle with an argument that the fees were "incentive pricing" rather than penalties since they wanted consumer behaviour to change and work within agreed facilities.

Extras

Are there other products – e.g. insurance, travel facilities, unit trusts, private banking – which might be offered to the customer? Are there other members of the family or other businesses in the group to which products can be sold? Cross-selling is becoming more and more important as more banks compete for the same customers. To a certain extent customers can be "locked in" by purchasing services from their bank. In addition banks are more able to target services to groups of existing customers as they have considerable information about their spending habits already.

In some cases the nature of the lending proposition will give rise to a need for the protection that insurance, in particular, can bring. Life assurance to cover a house mortgage loan is always advisable as dependants could be left with a loan to repay if the income earner dies with the loan outstanding. Similarly life cover for company directors who are vital to the success of a new investment is often offered by a banker.

Weaknesses of lending formulae

The weakness of using CAMPARI is that it can be backward looking. For business borrowing the lending officer also needs to go through forecasts of the accounts, including cash flow, for several periods ahead to see if the borrowing can be serviced, i.e. repayments made of part of the principal sum as well as payment of interest. For personal borrowers this also means judging the stability of a person's employment and their capacity to earn at the level needed to service the loan. Professionals such as solicitors or doctors can show an ability to earn high salaries easily but a production worker in an area of high unemployment may not, especially if fleeting overtime payments are needed to make the repayments.

In addition CAMPARI and ICE does not consider a very commercial feature of lending that other acronyms (such as PARSERS and 4C's) do. This is the relationship between the borrower and other customers. "PARSERS" includes Expediency as a feature and 4C's looks at Connections. Clearly a bank will not wish to sour its relationship with a good connected account by refusing a loan to, say, the managing director's son or daughter.

Personal credit scoring

This is a practice used to help lending decisions for personal borrowers. Credit scoring is routinely performed as soon as an account is opened, aiding the decision whether to issue a debit card immediately. Banks (or rather credit reference agencies[17]) update and augment the customer's score by analysing account behaviour once the account is running.

In basic credit scoring for a new borrower various characteristics of the potential borrower and the loan request are each given a rating or score. The numbers are then added up and read off against a range of risk probabilities. This range is calculated from past experience of the lender (see Figure 11.4).

Thus, a bank or building society may take a policy decision to reject all personal loan applications where there is more than a 10% chance of the loan not being repaid. The potential borrower's score will then be read across to this risk percentage, showing whether the risk is within the 10% acceptability level.

One benefit of credit scoring is that it is consistent and that its success (or otherwise) can be measured. In addition the "pass" mark can be altered up or down as the lending or marketing policy of the bank changes. Direct or internet banks use credit scoring extensively since they are unable to meet face to face with customers.

The scoring process indicates the level of risk associated with the proposition, not whether that particular loan will be a bad debt. Moreover, the scoring can always be overridden by a manager who takes other factors into consideration.

Although credit scoring criteria are designed to measure risk statistically they can be interpreted using the CAMPARI framework. CAMPARI seeks evidence of stability (length of time at an address); trustworthiness (occupation); other credit and monthly outgoings (ability to manage finances); and residential status (insurance in the form of assets).

In Appendix A at the end of this book you will find an example of a basic "static" credit scoring template and a case study that illustrates the principles of credit scoring.

---

17 Credit reference agencies operate worldwide and offer banks services of a quality that banks could not deliver themselves. By accepting information from banks and credit card companies on the basis of sharing it with others the CRA can augment the information available to a sole bank. Experian, based in Nottingham, is a major CRA and its website is well worth a visit.

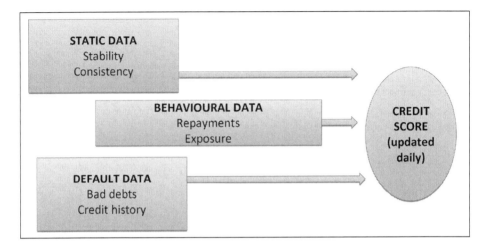

Figure 11.3: How credit scoring works

Scoring is often done by computer, with the results shown on the screen to the bank operative immediately. This is very convenient for branch-based transactions and also for direct banking services using the telephone. Applications will also be vetted via a credit bureau to reveal any county court judgments or bankruptcy orders in the past.

Scoring is also cheap to run. Per transaction the cost to the bank is minimal when compared to the traditional "relationship" approach where a bank officer would interview every applicant. In addition the whole system is scalable – it can be expanded to different products and branches or across platforms readily. Chapter 9 on delivery systems showed how important speed of decision making can be, especially on internet-based transactions.

And it works…..although banks may not spot problems early enough or filter out all risky loans at the outset those that use credit scoring for consumer products can show that the success rate in granting profitable loans that are repaid is consistently higher than the traditional "personal" method of credit appraisal.

In times of credit expansion or credit squeeze or to accommodate different risk appetites a bank can simply decrease or increase the "pass" score for certain products in order to filter out fewer or more "bads" as shown in Figure 11.4.

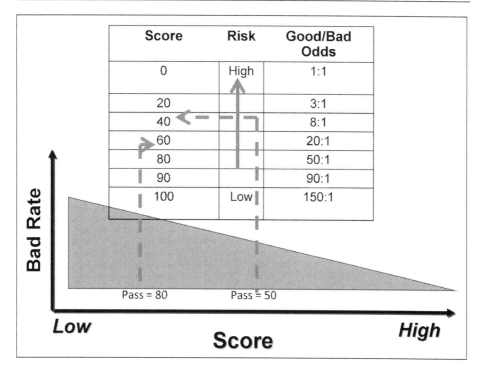

Score	Risk	Good/Bad Odds
0	High	1:1
20		3:1
40		8:1
60		20:1
80		50:1
90		90:1
100	Low	150:1

Figure 11.4: Credit scoring probabilities

Behavioural credit scoring will add to and amend the score as time goes on by reviewing such things as:

▶ the number of credit facilities open (banks share this information as well as the more negative data on default in an attempt to avoid borrowers becoming overstretched).

▶ the repayment record on each facility.

▶ missed repayments and by how much they were missed.

▶ court judgments for non-payment of debt since the credit was granted.

▶ bankruptcy.

It is possible to discover one's own credit score at any time by applying to a credit reference bureau. Genuine mistakes in the files can be rectified but a bad payment history cannot be hidden.

Overriding is possible, particularly if the potential borrower is part of an important business or family connection for the branch. For instance, it would be foolish to refuse a loan to a director of a large company banking with the branch or to the daughter of a very wealthy family, solely on the arithmetic of a computer.

Summary

This chapter has covered:
- The lending lifecycle
- Lending formulae
- CAMPARI and ICE considerations for credit assessment
- Personal credit scoring

Further reading and useful web links

Rouse, C. N., *Bankers' Lending Techniques*, 3rd Edition, (2011), Global Professional Publishing

Experian website at http://www.experian.co.uk/creditreport/

CHAPTER 12

Banking Securities

Objectives

After studying this chapter you should be able to:

- Discuss the importance of security.
- Explain some of the major factors involved in taking security.
- Describe some of the major forms of banking security.
- Explain the steps needed to take security.

Introduction

This chapter covers some key issues in the area of banking securities. This text does not have the scope to provide a definitive review of all of the different types of securities and the legal rules surrounding them but complements Chapter 11 on lending and further underlines the importance of an understanding of key legal principles.

The qualities of a good banking security are reviewed, explaining how bank policies and procedures reflect the legal and practical issues involved. A bank security form or charge form is actually a contract and so elements of contract law in the relevant jurisdiction must be understood before customers are asked to "sign on the dotted line". Failure to adhere to these principles can nullify the security and make it worthless for the bank.

This is followed by a summary of the key securities sought by banks from personal and business customers. This is followed by an overview of key procedural steps in the "perfection" of common securities.

As mentioned in the last chapter, security does not make a bad lending decision a good one but will ultimately reduce the risk of financial loss should the loan not be repaid. This will only be the case, however, if the legal and practical steps to "perfect" the security have been followed correctly.

The qualities of good banking security

Chapter 11 looked at the questions which should be asked by a lender to judge the credibility of a lending proposition, especially the stability and certainty of the primary source of repayment. In many cases the bank also seeks security (insurance in CAMPARI) as a secondary source of repayment should the primary one fail. Security protects the lender in case things go wrong.

In the USA and other parts of the world "security" is called "collateral". It is interesting to note that the term "collateral" is derived from the Latin for "side by side", emphasising that there are two contracts, one for the credit and one for the security.

For practical reasons banks prefer the type of assets where ownership can be evidenced by documents (certificates, deeds etc.). Without the relevant documents no transfer of ownership or sale is possible. This gives effective control over the asset to the person holding the documents.

Banks much prefer dealing with securities where ownership can be evidenced in this way rather than with "chattels" such as cars, plant and machinery or furniture. Chattels ownership is often evidenced by possession of the asset as documentary proof of ownership is not standardised. However valuable these assets may be, they cannot be charged or controlled as effectively as land, shares or life policies.

For business borrowers' assets that change in the course of business can be captured under a "floating charge". This type of charge is available in a number of legal jurisdictions

By contrast, a **finance company** will use cars or machinery as assets to support lending since the finance company retains ownership (but not physical possession) of the asset until it is paid for. There can be tax and cash flow advantages of this but it is not really security in a banking sense.

Another common security is the guarantee, given by an individual, jointly and severally or by a company. This is a promise to pay the bank should the borrower default. By itself it is a simple contract but has no real value until it is called upon. How certain can a bank be that the guarantor will pay the amount owed? Supporting guarantees with physical security is important.

The MAST Test

One method of judging the effectiveness of an asset as security is by using the MAST Test. In relation to assets held as security the mnemonic M.A.S.T stands for:
- **Marketability** (how readily can it be sold?)
- **Ascertainability of value** (how easy is it to value accurately?)
- **Simplicity of Title** (how easily can ownership be proved?), and
- **Transferability of Title** (how easily can the bank gain ownership so that it can sell the asset?

Land (especially domestic property) is said to be a good security and meets the requirements of the MAST Test:

▶ There is normally a good market for houses, especially in popular areas. Industrial premises or shops may be more difficult to sell as this can depend on the planning permission needed regarding the use of land and the state of the economy.

▶ In many economies house prices are easily ascertained by reference to professional surveyors and valuers or just by looking at similar houses in the vicinity (the so called "drive by" valuation.)

▶ In the UK Land Registration, guaranteed by the government since 1925, provides for a very simple way to find out who owns a particular plot of land and who has a mortgage over it. However in other jurisdictions the legal ownership of land and the rights enjoyed by the "owner" will vary (see Figure 12.1).

▶ Finally, transfer of title over land to a bank is effected through the mortgage deed or charge form. This provides for the transfer of ownership to the bank in case of default on the loan it secures. Of course, the bank must give back to the original owner any funds not needed to repay the loan (the surplus, if any). Once again rights to occupancy and protection for families in distress will vary between jurisdictions.

Figure 12.1: Real estate ownership in various countries

COUNTRY	EVIDENCE OF TITLE	TYPES OF TITLE AVAILABLE	STATE GUARANTEE OF TITLE	MORTGAGE REGISTER
Australia	Public register	Freehold/ leasehold	Yes	Yes
Brazil	Public register	Owner/ possessor	No	Yes
China	Only state ownership allowed	Compensatory grant for a number of years	No	On mortgage of compensatory grant
Denmark	Electronic public register	Full ownership (leasehold barely known)	Yes	Yes

COUNTRY	EVIDENCE OF TITLE	TYPES OF TITLE AVAILABLE	STATE GUARANTEE OF TITLE	MORTGAGE REGISTER
France	Written deeds and public registers	Full ownership and leasehold	No	Yes
Russian Federation	State register	Full ownership and leasehold	Not strong	Yes
United States	Written deeds and public registers	Freehold/ leasehold	No	Yes
United Kingdom	Electronic public register	Freehold/ leasehold	Yes	Yes

Summarised from Practical Law Company
(http://property.practicallaw.com/mjg/cre-mjg

Other physical assets such as antique furniture ("chattels"), however valuable, make a rather poor security:

▶ There is normally a good market for it.

▶ Valuation is often based on opinions of experts and there can be wide variations due to condition of the furniture, provenance etc.

▶ Title is evidenced by sales invoices but these are not official documents and can be forged. The furniture may be stolen.

▶ Transfer to the bank will be impossible if title cannot be confirmed.

Added to that – the bank cannot control the asset without locking it away and banks do not really want to do this on a regular basis.

Securities that fail the MAST Test but remain popular are the unsupported guarantee and the floating charge as we will see later in this chapter.

Advantages and disadvantages of taking security

The main advantage of taking security for a banker is that it reduces moral hazard risk. This is the risk that the borrower will alter the default risk of the loan after the money has been lent. If the borrower is set to lose a valuable asset because the risk of the loan changes he/she may be less inclined to change the risk profile. This is a form of moral pressure on the debtor. "**YOUR HOME MAY BE REPOSSESSED IF YOU DO NOT**

KEEP UP REPAYMENTS ON YOUR MORTGAGE, is a strong motivation and a vital part of credit advertising in the UK to ensure that the monthly mortgage payment is made.

A further advantage for some loans is that sale of the asset provides the primary repayment vehicle. Having the asset as security ensures that the sale proceeds go directly to the bank. Finally, security is "insurance" against external events such as death of the borrower or the borrower losing their job.

Taking security also has disadvantages as the legal process needed to "perfect" the security and make it watertight can be costly and delay the loan. This can make a bank's loans uncompetitive as another bank may lend the money without security at all. As a general rule borrowing below certain amounts will be agreed on an unsecured basis since the cost, competitive and time factors are too great and reduce the bank's profit on the deal.

Banks also need to maintain a good image and this can be tarnished when security called on, for example, when a company fails and the bank sells the factory premises to get repaid. Jobs can be lost and often the bank is blamed.

Finally it is thought that taking security can actually increase the moral hazard risks! If, say, a company director charges all company assets to the bank and supports the company with his own personal assets (house, shares or life policy) he may well think that he has nothing more to lose if the company fails and will take higher risks than he otherwise would.

Contract law and bank securities

In the same way that banks must ensure that accounts should only be opened for customers with legal capacity who fully intend to create a legal relationship with the bank so security contracts must ensure that the depositor cannot later avoid the contract due to some legal defect. This is particularly important since bank charge forms are complex and lengthy documents and often a third party (not the borrower) deposits the security to secure the account of the borrower. Legal cases in the UK have forced banks to advise security providers to use independent solicitors to assist in the execution of security documents.

Key problems that banks need to be aware of are: *Mistake, Misrepresentation and Undue Influence*. A full discussion of these factors is beyond the scope of this text and will vary from jurisdiction to jurisdiction.

Avoiding the legal pitfalls – a UK example

The UK legal case of *O'Brien v Barclays Bank plc* (1993) laid down rules for banks when taking security. In all cases **Independent Legal Advice (ILA)** should be offered and a note made if it is offered and not taken up. Independent legal advice, where the charge form is sent to the depositor's solicitor (not the bank's) for the document to be explained, witnessed and attested by the solicitor. This was further supported in *Royal Bank of Scotland v Etridge* (2001) which stipulated that in offering ILA a bank should make direct contact with the security provider to explain:

1. That the independent solicitor must confirm in writing that full explanation of the security documentation has been given;
2. That the purpose of 1 (above) is to ensure that the security provider knows that they are fully bound by what they sign;
3. That the choice of which solicitor to use must be that of the security depositor.

Bank practice has evolved to fulfil the above requirements so that when any security form is to be signed it will automatically be sent to a solicitor of the depositor's choice with the appropriate instruction regarding explanation, witnessing of signatures and other formalities such as appropriate registration and notification of the charge.

The protection that this affords is for the security depositor, so that they fully understand what they are signing and can refuse to sign if they wish and for the bank. The bank can be sure that if the "Etridge" system is followed the charge cannot be overturned later. At all times the bank must be aware of the possibility of *Mistake, Misrepresentation and Undue Influence* and do all in its power to avoid the opportunity for these to affect the security depositor's decision to sign.

For the retail banker seeking to reduce its cost/income ratio the use of ILA can reduce the requirement for in-house legal teams and securities experts. Legal costs of the exercise are borne by the borrower/security depositor and if the legal advice turns out to be flawed or misleading the bank cannot be held liable if it has followed the precedent of the Etridge case.

Key banking securities

As mentioned above there is a narrow range of assets that form good banking security. The scope of this text does not allow for a full description of the sometimes complex legal framework surrounding them but Figure 12.2 summarises their key features. As we will see, when it comes to creating a security over any asset, two aspects prevail – value and control. Good securities must have sustainable value and title documents need to be deposited with the bank.

Figure 12.2(a): Key banking securities

SECURITY	FEATURES
Land	◆ Relates to land and all buildings or erections on it.
	◆ May be subject to restrictions such as planning permissions or listed building status/preservation orders.
	◆ Most land is easy to value using professional valuers.
	◆ Most land in the UK is registered at a District Land Registry. Since the Land Registration Act of 2002 data relating to title, price paid, ownership and mortgages (but not size of loan) are available electronically, for a small fee at the Land Registry website.
	◆ Title to land is guaranteed by government (Land Registration Acts 1925 and 2002).
Life Policy	◆ Contractual agreement between a Life Office and an individual to pay a sum of money either on death only (Whole of Life policy) or on death or attainment of a certain age (Endowment policy) in return for payment of a regular premium.
	◆ Contracts are "of the utmost good faith" and can be void if the client lies or hides facts from the insurer.
	◆ Sum assured is actuarially assessed considering the probability of death. Funds are invested in equities/stocks until maturity.
	◆ Easy to value by reference to the Life Office or specialist market in endowment policies.
	◆ Whole of Life policies have no value unless death occurs.
	◆ Can be assigned to a bank via an assignment form (charge by way of security).
Guarantee and Indemnity	◆ This is a written undertaking to be liable for another person's debts.
	◆ The guarantor can provide tangible security to cover this liability.
	◆ The indemnity part of the guarantee means that it is valid even if the borrower is not contractually liable on the debt (e.g. he is a minor).

All of the above securities can be deposited by individuals, jointly, by partnerships or by companies. In addition the following can be deposited as security by companies:

Figure 12.2(b): Key banking securities

Debenture/ Floating Charge	◆ This type of charge covers all assets in a company balance sheet that are not charged elsewhere.
	◆ The company is free to deal with the assets in the normal course of business until the bank makes demand.
	◆ Notoriously difficult to value as assets change constantly.
	◆ As with most charges given by a company, it will be void unless registered at the Companies Registry. Registered charges rank ahead of unsecured creditors in most insolvency jurisdictions.
Fixed Charge on Book Debts	◆ This is the charge typically used by factors[1] as it allows a lender to control the proceeds of a company's book debts.
	◆ Lack of control of the debts can avoid the charge or downgrade it to a floating charge.

[18]In effect there is little that a bank cannot take as security but certain assets are easier to take than others. Most assets can have a fixed charge created over them (including goodwill, the value of trademarks etc) but these will be used only rarely.

The important thing to note is that each security has a legal definition, a separate legal framework within which it is developed, and a different set of specific criteria that must be considered before the security can be "perfected".

Valuation of security

Banks, as lenders, should view the security, in most cases, as a secondary form of repayment but, in order to ensure that repayment of a loan will be forthcoming, the security needs to have sufficient value.

The best types of securities have readily available market information, professional valuers, stable or rising values (as with life policies) but banks recognise that nothing is certain and that fluctuations in value can occur in the short term particularly.

To combat this banks employ "lending margins". These margins represent a buffer to absorb fluctuations in value, disposal costs and accrual of interest if a loan is

---

18 Factoring deals with debts owed to a company (assets). A factor will lend the company, say, 80% of the value of the debts immediately and then collect the debt in due course. The final 20% is paid, less interest, when the debt is collected. In this way the factor looks after the company's invoicing and debt collection mechanism too.

in default. Banks can also employ a "worst case" or "gone concern" valuation – where, for example the value of the asset is based on a liquidation value, as if the company or individual was insolvent and a sale had to be effected immediately.

An obvious use of lending margins is the domestic house mortgage These are known as **Loan to Value (LTV) ratios**. A bank may offer a house mortgage for a maximum 80% LTV, giving a 20% lending margin buffer. Typically house prices fall in a recession whilst loan defaults rise, so the most likely time that the security will be needed is when prices are falling. In some jurisdictions where consumer credit regulation is tight the government will set maximum LTVs for major asset purchases such as apartments and cars. Germany and Singapore are examples of regulation-based LTVs.

In a "gone concern" valuation assets covered by a floating charge, such as stock, will typically be valued at 10% or 20% of the value attributed in the company's accounts. Stock in an insolvent business may be unsaleable, damaged, subject to warranty etc. all of which reduce its realisable value. There may be exceptions, for example, the stock of a jewellery store could be valued at 70% or 80% since its intrinsic value will be based on the weight of precious metals.

Since 1995 UK house prices (on average) have risen by 161% (Land Registry). The years 2008-09 saw a fall of 15% and although there was a rise of 10% the following year prices have fallen back to 2008 values at the time of writing (2013). Regional differences occur with London often out-performing other regions in average value and price appreciation. In the US house prices were subject to an unsustainable bubble, fuelled by cheap loans, in the period before the credit crunch of 2007/08.

Bankers, especially in the short term, should not believe the old saying "As safe as houses".

Picking up from the "MAST Test" of security it is valuation that causes both guarantees and floating charges to be weaker securities than, say, land. The value of both guarantees and floating charges can be estimated but it is not until they are called upon that their true value emerges.

For a guarantee, unless supported by good security, the value relies on the individual's or company's ability to pay. It is easy to take a guarantee but much more difficult to realise it. Similarly with floating charges – required when a company is in financial trouble – the value will be limited by the disposal of stocks, running down of debtors, lack of maintenance of moveable assets etc. prior to the company's failure.

Just as with constant monitoring of lending, security valuations need to be updated regularly to avoid unwelcome surprises when the security is called upon.

Procedural steps in perfecting securities

Security in the form of land, life policies and floating charges must be taken correctly in order that it can be used where a borrower fails to make repayment of the advance.

Typically this is a legal and practical process. A simple mnemonic – DIVAN can help to remember the necessary steps in the security taking process:

- ▶ **D** – Deposit of title documents
- ▶ **I** – Inspection of title documents and searching
- ▶ **V** – Valuation of the asset
- ▶ **A** – Authorisation of the mortgage or charge
- ▶ **N** – Notification that a charge is held

D, A and N relate to the need for a bank to control the asset whilst V, naturally, relates to value. The I (investigation) factor has implications for both value and control.

Typical DIVAN considerations when taking UK land as security are summarised in Figure 12.3:

Figure 12.3: Typical considerations when taking UK land as security

STEP	CONSIDERATIONS
Deposit	◆ Are these the original deeds/certificates or duplicates?
	◆ Has the Land Registry detail been accessed and updated?
	◆ Are the deeds/certificates complete (i.e. are previous mortgages now repaid?)
Inspection	◆ Who owns the security? Who has legal rights of occupancy/legal interests in the property?
	◆ Are there any prior charges? If so, how much is outstanding and can this charge be subordinated to that of the bank?
	◆ What searches need to be made? Local searches can reveal mining works, rights of access, planning for re-development etc.
	◆ Do the providers have the power to create a mortgage? This can be an issue for corporate depositors although protection for third parties dealing with companies is good.
	◆ Are there any impediments to creating a charge? There may be covenants affecting the property regarding usage.
Valuation	◆ How much is the security worth? How stable is the value and how easy/costly is it to value?
	◆ For property the insurance value (in case of destruction and re-building) will be different to the market value or forced sale value.

STEP	CONSIDERATIONS
Authorisation	◆ Who must execute the security? Owners, those with an interest in the property and the mortgagee (lender) must authorise the security.
	◆ In case of corporate borrowers is a company seal needed?
	◆ Have signatories been formally identified to avoid forgery?
	◆ Has independent legal advice been offered and taken up?
Notification	◆ Does the charge require registration? In the UK the answer is "yes" for all legal charges over land.
	◆ Where should the charge be registered to protect it? Typically this will be in the appropriate District Land Registry but for corporate depositors this will include the Companies Registry.

Using the security

The final section in this chapter and this text deals with the final act within the banker/ customer relationship – where the borrower cannot or will not repay and the security must be relied upon. For business borrowers this may involve the liquidation of their business.

Through following the DIVAN procedure the bank will have put itself in a position to enforce the sale of the secured asset(s). Thus, the bank can act without the approval of the security depositor but will normally have given notice to them by making formal demand for the repayment of the loan outstanding.

In most jurisdictions the bank has a further duty – to ensure that it gets the best possible price for the asset(s) when the decision to sell is taken. There is normally no duty to wait until better prices emerge as this can often be wiped out by the continuing accrual of interest on the outstanding loan.

Where domestic property is concerned, repossession can lead to eviction of the borrower from their home. For a business it could mean job losses. Banks must take care to minimise the bad publicity that can accompany this type of enforcement action – reputational risk is at stake if the bank is seen to be too harsh or too soft.

Summary

This chapter has covered:
- ▶ The qualities of good banking security
- ▶ The advantages and disadvantages of taking security
- ▶ Some legal issues regarding the taking and using security
- ▶ Key features of common securities
- ▶ Generic procedures for perfecting security

Further reading and useful web links

Practical Law Company http://property.practicallaw.com/mjg/cre-mjg

Roberts G, (2013), *Law Relating to Financial Services*, 8th edn., Global Professional Publishing.

UK Land Registry h ttp://www.landregistry.gov/

Personal Lending – Credit Scoring

An investment opportunity

Singaporean Dong Ching Thian Christine (33) graduated from Singapore Management University (SMU) at the age of 22 with a first class degree in Finance. She immediately started work for UOB in the investment banking division and has risen to the level of senior analyst. Christine's annual salary exceeds S$120,000 (£60,000) basic and she regularly receives annual bonuses of S$50,000 (£25,000) based on her investment record.

Christine lives alone and rents a luxury apartment overlooking Marina Bay in Singapore. She has lived at the same apartment for four years.

As an employee, Christine banks with UOB but her savings account has always been at Riverside Bank. She has three credit cards with overall credit limits totalling S$100,000 (£50,000) and uses these regularly to travel on business and on holiday. Card balances are paid in full every month. In the past two years she has travelled to New York, Sydney, Paris and Rome on holiday and to Hong Kong, Beijing and Tokyo for business.

Over a short space of time Christine has saved her bonuses of S$200,000 (£100,000) and has begun to invest in corporate bonds and shares on her own account. Initially she invested in a portfolio of bonds and shares worth S$100,000 (£50,000). This grew in value to S$125,000 (£62,500). Last year, however, she added a further S$100,000 (£50,000) of her savings but investments fell and her total portfolio is now worth only S$210,000 (£105,000).

Through banking contacts Christine has identified a personal investment opportunity in Vietnam. The venture is new and relatively high risk but the rewards are potentially huge. She wishes to borrow S$500,000 (£250,000) to invest and expects that this will double in value within twelve months.

1. Based on the Riverside Bank Pte Ltd initial credit scoring template overleaf (see also Chapter 11) calculate/estimate the credit score attaching to Christine. What does bank guidance say about granting the loan?
2. Using CAMPARI would you come to a different conclusion?

Riverside Bank – Credit Scoring

Personal		
Home telephone?	YES	5
	NO / NOT KNOWN	0
Age	<18	0
	18 - 30	5
	30 – 50	7
	50 - 65	10
	>65	5
Marital status	Married	4
	Single	4
	Divorced	0
	Widowed	4
Dependents	YES	2
	NO/NOT KNOWN	4
Residential		
Years at current address	<2	0
	2 - 10	4
	>10	7
Residential status	Own	10
	Rent	0
	With parents	4
Equity	<50%	0
	>50%	4

Employment			
Occupation	See list		
Years with current employer	<2	0	
	2 - 10	4	
	>10	7	
Gross Annual Income	<S$20,000	0	
	S$20 - 40,000	4	
	S$40 - 60,000	7	
	>S$60,000	10	
How is salary paid?	Cash/Cheque	0	
	Direct to Bank	4	
Salary frequency	Weekly	0	
	Monthly	5	
	Other	0	
Banking			
Existing customer?	YES	10	
	NO / NOT KNOWN	0	
Debit card held?	YES	2	
	NO / NOT KNOWN	0	
Savings accounts?	YES	4	
	NO / NOT KNOWN	0	
Loans?	YES	2	
	NO / NOT KNOWN	0	
Credit cards/Charge cards	0	0	
	1-3	4	
	3-6	2	
	>6	0	

For NON CUSTOMERS ONLY

Singapore Citizen/ Permanent resident?	if NO - REFER		
Credit Register	CLEAR?	10	
		TOTAL	

Employment	
Professional	10
Managerial	7
Clerical	4
Manual	2
Student	10
Unemployed/ Housewife	0

Total scores	
>75	Grant loan/credit card/ Open account with overdraft
60 - 75	Refer loan/credit card to manager/Open account with debit card
40 - 60	Decline loan/credit card but open account
<40	Decline account*

NOTE

This is a fictitious credit scoring template designed for educational/illustrative purposes only. Riverside Bank is a fictitious organisation.

An investment opportunity – Some feedback

1. Although some interpretations may differ Christine's score is clearly above 75 (could be as high as 90) and so bank guidance would suggest that the loan be granted.

2. CAMPARI, however might suggest that it is too risky:

   C – No problems here and if behaviour on the bank account were taken into consideration this would look positive too.

   A – Christine has been relatively successful with her investments but has shown no previous ability to manage an investment of this size and risk.

   M – The proposition is for 100% financing – there is no contribution from Christine and so the whole of the risk falls on the bank.

   P – Speculative investment in an overseas territory is a proposal fraught with risk and potential problems such as repatriation of income streams and repayment of the investment, not to mention political changes that could block repatriation.

A – The amount, in relation to her ability, previous experience, assets and security is far too large.

R – Repayment is from speculation and the nature of the underlying investment is unclear. As investors with Bernard Madoff discovered, if it seems too good to be true (investment returns) then it probably is too good to be true.

I – Christine has an investment portfolio currently worth S$210,000. Fluctuations in equities prices can be large and so a lending margin of 40% – 50% would be sensible. This would mean that there is insufficient security to cover the investment save for the investment itself. If the investment turns out to be problematic then the security value will fall too.

Holiday Flats – Business Lending Proposition

Holiday flats

Tania Cunningham, 45, Marketing Director of your bank's largest corporate client, UK Bus plc, sends you the following email message requesting an interview. Tania does not bank with you at present but you are aware that she receives a salary in excess of £100,000 per annum and owns a substantial shareholding in UK Bus plc.

From: tania.cunningham@ukbus.co.uk

To: lending@countryside.co.uk

Sent: Monday, this week 1:02 PM

Subject: Possible Loan

I'd like to discuss borrowing £200,000 to purchase a block of eight seaside apartments in Brighton. The price is fairly low because the seller is a member of my family and the apartments need some repair before they can be let out to summer visitors.

The apartments will be worth £350,000 on the open market once repaired and I intend use my own resources to fund the repairs, which I estimate will cost £50,000.

My intention is to let the apartments next summer from which I should receive £40,000 in rent. After the summer season I will sell four of the renovated apartments and use the funds to repay the bulk of the borrowing.

Do you need any more information?

Tania

REQUIRED

Using the CAMPARI system, consider the key information that you would ask Tania to provide.

Holiday flats – Some feedback

The Tania Cunningham lending proposition presents an excellent opportunity to "get inside" a transaction and review it from a banking perspective.

Any decision to lend will, of course, depend on bank policy and guidelines but due diligence using CAMPARI should reveal the following priority areas:

Repayment

As the bulk of the loan is an open-ended bridging loan (no firm buyer yet) repayment is vitally important. Good approaches will stress the certainty of repayment through questions such as:

- "Are the valuations and projections valid?"
- "Have projections and quotes been checked independently?"
- "Have all the costs of renting apartments been included?"
- "How much will be repaid from the sale?"

Many banks may want to take a full £200,000 repayment on the sale but this reckons without the motivations that Tania has for entering the purchase in the first place. Better approaches might deal with the residual loan after the refurbishment or even treat the proposition as TWO loans from the outset. Clearly there would need to be a repayment schedule set up for the residual loan (say over 15-20 years, repayable from income from the flats).

The payment of interest on the outstanding advance also needs to be considered as a bank would wish to see interest covered from the outset. Rental income could pay interest post refurbishment but Tania's substantial income could be relied upon in the initial stages.

Ability

Tania's skill and experience in this field is also an important priority. Has she done anything like this before? Has she the time available to manage this and her full-time job? Better lenders will query the market for flats, the level of rent, the possibility that flats would be vacant for some of the time and whether the renovations would be ready in time for the summer season. Using a local agent may be costly but necessary if expertise is to be used to fill the flats and gain the promised income.

Means/Margin

This tests Tania's commitment to the project. £50,000 is a substantial investment for any individual but where does it come from? If the funds are borrowed then her commitment would not be that great. If the funds are from savings or the sale of UK Bus plc shares her commitment would be seen to be greater.

Amount

Although the purchase price may be certain the costs of renovation are estimated and may require further borrowing if the estimate is too low. Independent estimates for the renovation work need to be obtained.

Insurance (security)

The bank does need to be protected in this transaction in case things go wrong. As the property forms the bulk of the repayment it would be sensible to take it as security. Suggesting additional security such as Tania's house or shares is over-cautious and, possibly not commercial. Competitor banks would do this deal with just the apartments as security.

Where security cover was felt to be too slim (loan £200k, auction value of flats, say, £250k – rather than the projected £350k when renovated) the bank could reformulate the deal as follows:

1. Lend £150,000 immediately and get Tania to use her £50,000 to purchase the property.
2. Agree a refurbishment schedule (one or two apartments at a time) and release funds in tranches of £10,000 (up to £50,000) to pay for refurbishments when they have been completed or stages have been reached.

In this way the value of the property should rise as the loan rises and the bank's money is not at risk.

But – what if the property market continues to be difficult and the glamour of Brighton fades in the minds of holidaymakers? A substantial lending margin is needed based on sensible valuations.

Character

As this transaction will be secured it is Tania's ability to manage rather than her Character that is important. A good credit history should be sought but it is unlikely to reveal a transaction of this size. Similarly a glance at her bank statements will not add much relevant information. Character is important but not as vital as repayment or security to get right. An additional point is that she has influence at a high level within a major customer of the bank and so giving her a hearing is essential – even if the answer is "no" at the end of the day.

Purpose

Property speculation (even on such favourable terms) is not always favoured by banks. Property issues (secondary banking crisis in the 1970s and the sub-prime mortgage problems of recent years) carry higher levels of risk – that's why it is called "speculation". However, the objective of the transaction is to add value and is perfectly reasonable as a "side venture" for an already wealthy customer.

& ICE

Most banks would provide a detailed breakdown of interest and fees for the deal. Tania could expect to pay between 3 and 6% over the base rate or LIBOR depending on the level of repayment risk perceived.

A fee of 1% of the loan (£1,500 or £2,000) would be a realistic fee. The loan would involve a good deal of work and monitoring by the bank and the fee would need to reflect this.

Other relevant services such as insurance could also be offered.

Note: UK Bus plc is a fictitious company devised solely for the purposes of this illustration.

Zoë Young – Micro-business Lending Proposition

Your branch of Countryside Bank plc has held the account of Zoë Young ever since she started her studies at Anytown University. Zoë graduated with a first class degree in Photographic Studies in 2010 and then trained with a prestigious studio in London.

Zoë's account has always been conducted satisfactorily, even whilst an undergraduate, and, due to her generous parents and her talent for taking and selling photographs to the media, she had never needed to borrow or take out a student loan. Whilst training in London she continued to support herself from freelance earnings; several of her pictures have been used by national magazines and her fame is beginning to grow.

You have arranged an appointment with Zoë to discuss an expedition that she wishes to organise. Her initial letter to you shows that she seeks to borrow £20,000 to cover equipment purchase and flights to Africa for herself and an assistant. Once in Africa Zoë will take wildlife photographs, marketing them around the world to journals, publishers and websites.

REQUIRED

Before Zoë comes to the bank for an interview you must reflect on the questions you will ask her to help you make a decision. What key questions and considerations will you have in mind?

Download a suggested answer from author's website at:

http://tinyurl.com/keithpond

Index